D1535175

ULSTER'S OTHER POETRY
Rhymes and Songs of the Province

JOHN WYSE JACKSON lives in County Wexford. Among his books are *We All Want to Change the World: A Life of John Lennon*, *The Rare Oscar Wilde* and *Flann O'Brien at War* (which was illustrated by Hector McDonnell).

HECTOR McDONNELL lives in County Antrim. One of Ireland's leading artists, he has written several books (*A History of Dunluce*, *The Wild Geese of the Antrim Mac-Donnells*, etc.) and illustrated others, such as Raymond Calvert's *The Ballad of William Bloat* and John Campbell's *Saturday Night in York Street*.

THE EDITORS have also worked together on *Ireland's Other Poetry: Anonymous to Zozimus* and *Dublin's Other Poetry: Verses and Songs of the City*. If you know of any further examples of 'Other Poetry' that deserve to be rescued, they would be delighted to hear from you via the publisher or by email at irelandsotherpoetry@hotmail.com. Such discoveries feature on a web page, http://irelandsotherpoetry.spaces.live.com.

The book is dedicated, with love, to
Coll and Hannah McDonnell and to Conor and Adam Jackson.

ULSTER'S OTHER POETRY
Rhymes and Songs of the Province

Edited by John Wyse Jackson
and Hector McDonnell

THE LILLIPUT PRESS
DUBLIN

First published 2009 by
THE LILLIPUT PRESS
62–63 Sitric Road, Arbour Hill
Dublin 7, Ireland
www.lilliputpress.ie

ISBN 978 1 84351 160 1

10 9 8 7 6 5 4 3 2 1

A CIP record for this title is available
from The British Library.

Set in 11.5 on 14pt Dante by Marsha Swan
Printed in England by MPG Books, Bodmin, Cornwall

Contents

(Verses are arranged alphabetically by author or, if anonymous, by title.
Inverted commas denote working titles supplied for this edition.)

Introduction

Like many another desperate person searching for something to say I find myself groaning and gazing out of the window. The little north Antrim glen I am looking at sweeps away down to the sea, and in the distance, bobbing on a watery horizon, are two blobs of land. I can never see those blobs without grinning, inwardly at least, as I remember an uncle who, when told what they were called, remarked, 'Ah, perfect names for guests at a grand Scottish house party, "the old Mull of Kintyre and his daughter Ailsa Craig."'

Those Scottish blobs often look so near that you cannot believe they belong to a different country, and I have only to listen to any of my neighbours talking to know how close we in fact are. Words and phrases that tripped off Robbie Burns' tongue are still in daily use, though to people from other corners of Ireland they sound just as foreign as they do to any visiting English. Local culture continues undeterred here, in spite of its incomprehensibility to outsiders, and farmers still go onto the moss to cut their peats with a loy, or come back after a bad day's wroughting on the land drenched in clabber to their oxters after falling into a sheugh.

> There was a wee fella frae Clough
> Who was fu', and fell in till a sheugh ...

Most of the verses in this book are the work of poets proudly aware of how special, and different, their particular corners of Ulster are, when compared to anywhere else. Inevitably, even though I am a fellow Ulsterman, many of them refer to things I have never really known: to wartime bombings, to university idylls, to academic literary disputes, to Belfast streets and shipyards, to unpleasant voyages, to incidents in 'the Troubles', to linen looms and indeed to digging for gold. But even though the localities and times of these poems may lie far from my own experiences, in their very familiar tones and twists and accents, they reward me with a strong sense of home.

There is, I believe, in Ulster a very particular and effective brand of humour – something that might be described as 'the bull's memory of the china shop' (to rip out of context a brilliant line by the Ulster poet Tess Hurson). My own earliest experiences of the power of this poetical fun came from children's parties, where one or other of our beloved local poets would inevitably stand up to do his party piece. One of them, Robert Morrow, who was my best adult friend in those days, would always terrify us with a versified account of going to the dentist to have a bad tooth pulled out, and its inevitable grisly climax:

> Hold on there Robert
> It's out! It's out!

Having finished that performance Robert would put a box of matches on the floor, stand up straight, carefully balance a full glass of water on the top of his head, slowly slide down until he was lying on the ground, clamp his remaining teeth round the matchbox and get up again without spilling a drop. It was a time blessed with as many such lyrical pleasures as anyone could ever hope for.

As we worked on this collection, many hours were enjoyably spent by John Wyse Jackson, my co-compiler, and myself, rummaging through long-forgotten books and magazines in dusty libraries, but an equal amount of energy was devoted to exploring personal poetry collections, and in particular one assembled by another great local entertainer, Mat Meharg. I maligned his family abominably in our first volume, *Ireland's Other Poetry*, imagining that a surviving brother had locked all his poems in a cupboard and would let no one near them. In fact it is his sister who still lives in his house, and when I summoned the courage to visit her she was totally delighted to let me spend as much time as I wished with Mat's boxes of poems, and indeed she even appears to have forgiven me my extreme silliness in telling my fanciful tale.

To my surprise, with one possible exception none of the poems in this unique archive of Ulster wit was by Mat himself; he had rather spent his time collecting and reciting the poems of other people. Without his hard work this book would be nothing like as good as it is, and so in partial thanks I reproduce here an anonymous ode to Mat who, when he wasn't entertaining the locality with extracts from his personal anthology, became the local taxi firm, cycle shop and garage. I suspect that the anonymous author was actually Mat himself, but whether he was or he wasn't I can just see him charming every pretty girl who caught his eye at a party by reciting it, and making her feel that he had composed it on the spot just for her. (The acronyms refer to his sometime employers, a long-vanished firm of local fuel providers.)

> I'm M.S. Meharg of the E.D.C.P.
> I'm fond of the lassies and a wee cuppa tea.
> One day down at Esso House I chanced for to see
> A bonny wee lass wi' a glint in her e-e.
> Says I to that lassie will ye walk for a while,
> I'll buy you a bonnet so we'll do it in style,
> My stripes are the Esso of E.D.C.P.
> She looked at me shyly, and then said to me:
>
> An Esso Boy for me, an Esso Boy for me,
> If you're no an Esso Boy, you're no use to me.
> The Shell boys are bra, Lebites an a',
> But the smilin' wee Esso Boy's the pride o' them a'.
>
> I courted that lass neath an oak tree,
> I made up my mind she was fashioned for me,
> Soon I was thinking how nice it would be
> If she joined up in the Esso wi' me.

The day we were wed the grass was so green
An' the sun shone so bright as the light horiseen.
Now we've two bonny lassies who sit on her knee
While she sings the song that she once sang to me:

An Esso Boy for me, an Esso Boy for me,
If you're no an Esso Boy, you're no use to me.
The Shell boys are bra, Lebites an a',
But the smilin' wee Esso Boy's the pride o' them a'.

Very many of the verses in this book have a similar strength and vitality, because they were composed by Ulster people who simply wished to entertain other members of the community. In their various ways they amply compensate for any absence of purely 'literary' ambition with their robustness, pithy wit and good common sense. May this book give as much pleasure as any of those local childhood parties I still remember so vividly. That wonderful figure, Jimmy Kelly, the local road mender who was the composer of several poems in *Ireland's Other Poetry*, and who appears in a poem in this one, would, I believe, have approved of it. Verse was inextricably part of Jimmy's daily life. Often enough he would start proclaiming in rhyme as soon as he saw you coming, and always he created laughter. One day the local doctor saw him at work while driving along the coast road, and stopped to introduce him to his newly arrived and very attractive nurse – who had only taken the job because she was already walking out with another of the locals. So, Doctor Brennan wound down the window and began, 'Jimmy can I introduce you to …' but before he could say any more Jimmy looked in through the open window at them and pronounced,

You may sit beside her but you must not touch her,
For she's engaged to MacAllister the butcher.

Hector McDonnell

William Allingham

*Though he is sometimes rather lazily called 'The Bard of Ballyshannon',
William Allingham (1824–89) is hardly thought of as an Ulster poet at all.
He once summed up the problems of his own nationality in a succinct verse:*

> An Englishman has a country,
> A Scotchman has two,
> An Irishman has none at all—
> And doesn't know what to do.

*A native of Donegal, in early life Allingham wrote 'traditional' ballads
to airs by local musicians for sale as penny broadsheets. After many years as an
Irish customs official, he left the airy mountains and rushy glens for England,
where he edited magazines and gossiped with many of the great figures of
Victorian literature. Alfred, Lord Tennyson, then Poet Laureate, became a good
friend – despite his assertion that 'Kelts are all mad furious fools!'*

*In 1851 the final volume of John O'Donovan's English translation of the
Annals of the Four Masters appeared, and Allingham wrote this spirited
précis of the book, no doubt confirming Tennyson's opinion of the wild Irish.
The lines were eventually published in By the Way (1912), a posthumous
collection of the poet's fragments and notes.*

IRISH ANNALS

MacMurlagh kill'd Flantagh, and Cormac killed Hugh,
Having else no particular business to do.
O'Toole killed O'Gorman, O'More killed O'Leary,
Muldearg, son of Phadrig, killed Con, son of Cleary.

Three show'rs in the reign of King Niall the Good
Rain'd silver and honey and smoking red blood.
Saint Colman converted a number of pagans,
And got for his friars some land of O'Hagan's;
The King and his clansmen rejoiced at this teaching
And paused from their fighting to come to the preaching.
The Abbot of Gort, with good reason no doubt,
With the Abbot of Ballinamallard fell out,
Set fire to the abbey-roof over his head,
And kill'd a few score of his monks, the rest fled.
The Danes, furious pirates by water and dry-land,
Put boats on Lough Erne and took Devenish Island;
The Monks, being used to such things, in a trice
Snatching relics and psalters and vessels of price,
Got into the Round-Tower and pull'd up the ladder;
Their end, for the Danes lit a fire, was the sadder.
Young Donnell slew Rory, then Dermod slew Connell;
O'Lurcan of Cashel kill'd Phelim his cousin
On family matters. Some two or three dozen
Of this Tribe, in consequence, killed one another.
MacFogarty put out the eyes of his brother
James Longthair, lest James should be chosen for chief.
At Candlemas, fruit-trees this year were in leaf.
King Toole, an excitable man in his cups,
Falls out with King Rorke about two deerhound
    pups,
And scouring the North, without risking a battle
Burns down all the houses, drives off all the cattle;
King Rorke to invade the South country arouses,
Drives off all the cattle, burns down all the houses.
If you wish for more slaughters and crimes and
    disasters
See, *passim*, those annalists called 'The Four
    Masters'.

Anonymous

If Allingham's first interest was in folksong, so too, generations later, was Richard Hayward's (1892–1964). This now half-forgotten Ulsterman was probably at heart an actor, but he was also an enthusiastic singer, film-maker, harper, folklore collector and anthologist, and a fine and companionable writer of travel books such as The Corrib County *(1943) and* Border Foray *(1957).*

In 1924, Hayward summed up for the Ulster Review *the essence of what he called the 'Ulster Quality': 'The hard commonsense. The hatred of pose. The terrific sense of humour. The pride of race. The belief that an Ulster man has no business with a Chelsea accent.'*

He came across the following enjoyable survival in Co. Cavan, and included it in his 1925 anthology, Ulster Songs and Ballads of the Town and the Country. *It demonstrates all the attributes required for Ulsterness, and should on no account be recited in a Chelsea accent.*

THE ASS AND THE ORANGEMAN'S DAUGHTER

In the County Tipperary, at a place called Longford Cross,
There dwelt one Thomas Brady, who had a stylish ass;
But he was seized by heresy and canted was for tithes,
And on Forren's Hill you'll see these news; and his name was
    Henry Boyd.

This ass was sold by auction for a monstrous sum of debt
And was purchased by an Orangeman, which caused him for to fret;
For he tied him with a cable, and fettered him across,
And confined him in a stable with neither food nor grass.

For three long days he was kept there with not one bit to ate,
And on the morning of the fourth in walks the daughter Kate;
She opens a large Bible and begins to read, with hope,
And says she: Me paypish donkey now, you must deny the Pope.

If you'll become an Orangeman and join King William's host,
And deny infallibility and all that kind of boast,
You shall be set at liberty, and feed on oats and hay,
And decent prayer you yet may hear on every Sabbath day.

My charming lass, replied the
    ass, the truth I now must tell,
But first of all I'll ask you for
    to kindly go to hell;
I never will deny the sacred
    emblem of the Cross,
For I wear it on my
    shoulder though
    I'm only just an ass.

Miss Kate she frowned and answered,
    saying: How dare you me refuse!
    I'll make you suffer very sore before
        you do get loose.

I'll whip your hide until
    your side looks like a
    piece of beef,
And where's the paypish
    squirt-boy that dare come
    till your relief?

This Orange lass she seized a stick
    to knock the donkey down,
When a multitude of asses full
    soon gathered there around;
And they tore her flounces into
    rags, and set the donkey free,

To show this Orange termagant
    they'd fight for liberty.

5

Anonymous

*Purists may point out that the verses below violate our working definition of
'Other Poetry', since they have neither rhymes nor a regular metre. However,
they make up for it in so many other ways that it would be foolish indeed to
exclude them on a technicality.*

*Under the unidentified initials 'B.S.', the lines appeared in the autumn
of 1937 in the* New Northman, *a magazine produced by the students of
Queen's University, Belfast. With a touch of gentle satire, the author presents
the social and religious allegiances of Protestant Belfast, a now vanished
milieu that seems closer to the nineteenth century than to the eve of World
War II.*

The poem was inspired by a letter to the Belfast Press *from the Ulster
Evangelical Protestant Society. Following protests, a planned Sunday Concert
conducted by Sir Thomas Beecham had just been cancelled. The Society
was 'delighted to see how well the Police Committee of the Corporation
has gauged the real attitude of the best thought in Ulster to the question of
Sabbath Desecration'.*

THE ATHENS OF THE NORTH, 1937

In the year of our Lord one thousand nine hundred and seven
    and thirty
There was convened at Belfast, Metropolitan City of Ulster,
A large and distinguished concourse of people,
Who had assembled together to witness against the desecration
    of Sunday,
And to proclaim their will to the world, but more particularly to
    the Northern Government and Belfast Corporation.

Mr. Saml. Jas. McIlhagga kindly presided,
And Rev. Obadiah McCusker led the Praise.

The principal speaker was Rev. Clugston Maconkey,
Who spoke with regret of secular music broadcast on Sunday,
And, denouncing the practice of Sabbath joy-riding,
Drew a grave picture of beaches strewn with bottles of whiskey
(Empty, of course), and of motors in serried arrays
Wherein couples lay clasped in illicit embraces.
And although they had closed the Gallery of Art and Museum,
Where was the use if the workers got railway excursions?
And now they were menaced by Sir Thomas Beecham
And his so-called London Symphony Orchestra.
A speaker who followed referred to the fate of Gomorrah,
Remarking that righteousness ever exalteth a nation;
But nowadays even the Loyal, Imperial Province
Had deserted the Bible, and wallowed in sin and iniquity.
The discussion concluded, the Chairman submitted a motion,
Which was passed with applause, and conveyed to the
     proper authorities,
And which duly appeared in the Press
(Condensed, and its grammar amended).

The Misses Minnie McCann and Sadie
     Mahaffy
Thereupon kindly consented to sing,
With Mr. Albert McClurg, L.R.C.M.
Presiding at the harmonium.
'O God, our help in ages past'
Was fervently sung by all present;
And the proceedings were terminated
By the strains of the National Anthem.

And there were present:
Holy Rollers,
Little White Ribboners
(With at least three Temperance Queens),
All the Belfast Vigilance Committees,
The League of Patriots, and the Band of Hope;
Also the Council of the Ruling Elders' Union,
Several Aldermen and Councillors of the Corporation,
Delegates from numerous Total Abstinence Orange Lodges,
Likewise the Jubilee Protestant Defence Association;
And as well there were representatives
Of the Peculiar People,
British Israel,
The Anti-Popery League,
And the Purity Brigade.
The Ulster Unionist Labour
    Association arrived in a taxi
(Attired as usual in full evening
    dress).
There was also the Ulster
    Evangelical Protestant
    Society,
And of course
The Little Flock.

George Barnett

Born in the Sixtowns, Co. Derry, George Barnett (1876–1965) was a reluctant farmer. In his spare time he wrote for the local papers on the history, geography, botany, and folklore of the Sperrin Mountains. His verses, a more private pleasure, did not appear in book form until 1980, when a little volume called The Wee Black Tin: Poems from Ballinascreen *was prepared for the Ballinascreen Historical Society by Graham Mawhinney and Jennifer Johnston, with an introduction by Seamus Heaney.*

Readers who are dairy farmers may find this poem instructive in cases of 'slip-tail', a frequently fatal weakness of the spine in cattle.

KELLY'S 'SLIP-TAIL' COW

O, Lissan is a lovely spot and very well it's known,
It stands in County Derry, and convenient to Tyrone.
Churchtown is lying near at hand, and somewhat
    further o'er
You may find that lovely village that the folk call Moneymore.

Now if you come down Lissan way, in need of drink or grub,
You had better call at Kelly's, for he has a famous pub.
You will be sure to find it, for he keeps good drink galore,
And you'll see the name of Kelly just a bit above the door.

Now Kelly has a famous cow, a springer too the same,
And he was looking forward to the handling of the cream
Till he found her down one morning and was very much surprised
To see her lying helpless, completely paralysed.

He grabbed her quickly by the tail and found that it was slack,
Thinks he, 'It's slip-tail she has got, and working in the back.
I'll send for brave McCully, he's a very useful man,'
But the case it was quite baffling and the cow she seemed so bad.

Now Kelly he bethought himself of an old-time country cure,
And hurried off to the Sixtowns, the same for to secure.
He had to race about a bit, which made his heart feel sore,
Till at last he was directed to a place called Tobermore.

Soot, rue and garlic was the stuff, the stuff for which he came,
Saltpetre too and butter, for the blending of the same.
Likewise a little salt as well, and a handful of goose dung,
To make the plaster hold on fast until the work was done.

The neighbours heard about the case and came the cow to view,
They wanted to help Kelly for he was their neighbour too.
McCracken he was early there, likewise brave John Cahoon,
John Conlon too and Matthew, and all in the best of tune.

Now John Cahoon the plaster made, and that with a big knife,
The rest kept well away from him, being frightened for their lives,
And Kelly than took up the blade to give the tail a score,
And they tied the plaster on to stick, as if for evermore.

But the plaster quickly did its work, and the cow got on her feet,
And Kelly took them to the bar and gave them all a treat.
So they gave three cheers for Kelly, sure I think I hear them now,
Oh they gave three cheers for Kelly, aye, and likewise for the cow.

Francis Boyle

*During the century after 1750, workers in Ulster's domestic weaving trade
produced between them an estimated seventy books of verse. This by-product
of the industry was presumably inspired by the solitary nature of the job,
coupled with the regular rattle of shuttle and loom. In an important work
of literary archaeology,* Rhyming Weavers and other Country Poets of
Antrim and Down *(1974), the late John Hewitt revisited many of these
fascinating figures. In this book we can sample only a few.*

*The first is Francis Boyle of Gransha, near Comber, Co. Down, whose
poems were issued in 1811. He hinted at how the process worked, as his
thoughts fell into step with the rhythm of his labours:*

> When I am weaving on my loom
> I think upon my darling
> Though she resides in Moira Town
> And I live in Kilwarlin.

*Boyle was a loyal Tory, and as one of the 'Auld Licht' Presbyterians,
would allow no flexibility in creed or interpretation:*

> On proper subjects still you fix
> The church and state you never mix

Nor dip so deep in politics
About the Throne
As clergymen of other sects
That I have known.

Nevertheless, like many of the weavers, he fully appreciated the surreal and the funny sides of life.

from THE COAL HOLE

Frae Newtownards three miles or four
Near to Mount Stewart on the sea shore
A man does wi' his auger bore
    An' ither tools
Five hunner feet perhaps an' more
    In search o' coals.

In Mexico or rich Peru
Whare they find gold and silver too,
There's nae sic slavish wark to do
     In raisin' ore;
Nae beds o' freestane to pierce through
     Nor holes to bore.

But here, far distant frae the line
We hae nae gowd or siller fine,
Our metal's o' a coarser kind,
     Baith lead and coal,
While copper, brass or
   iron fine
     Lies near the pole.

While one mounts in an air balloon
To reconnoitre every town,
Ithers survey the county Down
     To map the roads;
This man does drive his auger down
     To the Antipodes.

But will this miner niver stap
Nor winter mak' him shut his trap,
Nor haul the tackle frae the tap
     O' the tall trees,
Till down his tools go wi' a slap
     I' the South Seas? ...

Harry T. Browne

Harry T. Browne (1877–1973) became known throughout the province for his writings in the Belfast Telegraph *and elsewhere. 'The Wong' comes from his collection,* The Dancing Men and Other Verses *(1950), published under his pseudonym, 'John o' the North'.*

THE WONG

The principal joy of Sir Adderly Brown
Was shooting at things and bringing them down.
I met him in High Street early in May,
And said to him, 'Adderly, whither away?'
'I'm thinking,' he said, 'of popping along
And having a shot at the Spotted Wong.'

 – Now the Wong, in case you may not have
    heard,
Is partly a beast and partly a bird,
And it flies, that is, if it flies at all,
Over the jungles of Senegal.
Its feet are webbed and the natives say
That its eggs are full of vitamin A
(An error here, for it seems to me
They are probably thinking of vitamin B).
Its wings are tipped with a yellowish fur,
And it's neither exactly a him nor a her
(A private matter, of course, for the Wong,
And we merely mention it *en passant*.)

Sir Adderly kissed his fond Mamma
And sailed for the shores of Africa;
And the latest news that has come to hand
Is of bones that bleach in the desert sand;

For it seems that a lion leaped from its den
And bit Sir A. in the abdomen,—
In fact it appears to have bitten him twice,
So the details are naturally far from nice.—
So the Wong still flies, if it flies at all,
Over the jungles of Senegal,
Awaking the swamp with its plaintive cry
And disturbing the hipp-o-pot-a-mi.

Anonymous

*Apparently, the gentle verses below, which were published in 1898 in the
Derry Journal, 'enjoyed considerable popularity as a sing-song of a summer
evening among railway trippers from Derry'. Among those mentioned along
the way is the King of Tory Island, whose hereditary post, held with the 'con-
sensus of the islanders', is said to date back to the sixth century. His realm
lay some nine miles north-west of the Donegal coast.*

THE BUNCRANA TRAIN

Some people like to have a drive
Whilst others like a row,
Young people getting up in life
A-courting they will go.
But if the evening does keep fine
And does not threaten rain,
Sure I'd prefer a trip to Fahan
On the Buncrana Train.

Chorus:
For Crockett he's the driver,
And Bonner is the guard,
And if you have a ticket
All care you can discard.
Let you be fop or 'summer swell',
To them it's all the same,
For every man must pay his fare
On the Buncrana Train.

For localists, provocalists,
And those that like to sing,
I'm sure McGarvey he'll be there
To play the Highland Fling.
As for singing or for dancing
To them it's all the same,
For he's the sole 'musicianer'
On the Buncrana Train.

We pass Bridgend, reach Burnfoot,
And there we give a call
To view that ancient city
And its Corporation Hall.
The King of Tory Island
Is a man of widespread fame,
His Royal Carriage is attached
To the Buncrana Train.

We go to Fahan to have a 'dip'
And stroll along the strand,
Then up the road to have a cup
Of coffee at the Stand,
The Barmaid she is charming,
With her you can remain
Until it's time for to go back
On the Buncrana Train.

James Campbell

Born in Carncastle, Co. Antrim, James Campbell (1758–1818) was another of the weaver poets. Both a United Irishman and a Freemason – not then a rare combination – he had all his poems confiscated when he was arrested in 1798. Though they were never returned, many of the ones he wrote over the next two decades were issued in book form to help his widow and his seven children after he died. (Sadly, others were 'judiciously suppressed' by a local schoolmaster, and have not survived.)

The verses below are taken from that volume, The Posthumous Works of James Campbell of Ballynure *(1820); winningly, they suggest an equation between belief and breakfast.*

from THE EPICURE'S ADDRESS TO BACON

O Fortune! thou hast been propitious,
As I on bacon am voracious—
To worship't would be superstitious,
    Or I would try it;
For, Lord! it is the most delicious
    Soul of diet.

My tripes they are completely swampit,
Nae aches nor pains my joints since crampit,
Wi' fervour I cry, Lord be thankit,
    Each day I dine;
I revere the power on matter stampit
    The form of swine.

Nae animal in all creation
Deserves so much my approbation,
It keeps my tripes in a right station,

Without crack or chasm;
'Tis of mair use to my salvation
    Than holy chrism.

I like swine's grease, some think it odd,
I scarce prefer the grace of God;
They sell their pigs to chiels abroad,   *fellows*
    For yellow coin;
The Devil o'er them ride rough-shod,
    Ere they get mine.

Some like their spirits up to cheer ,
With good strong whiskey, or brown beer,
Some like their brains for to keep clear,
    By wine applying;
Nae music ever charmed my ear,
    Like pork a frying.

John Campbell

John Campbell was born in Belfast in 1936. He grew up in Sailorstown, the close-knit community around York and Dock Streets, which he has chronicled in both verse and prose. The younger generation may not always appreciate the particular charms of an area, however, as the following short poem suggests. Written in 1967, it was published in his first collection, Saturday Night in York Street *(1982) – where Hector's illustration on this page originally appeared.*

THE PLACE

'Sailorstown, is this it?' said the young lad to his dad.
'Stretching all around you,' said the father to his lad.
'It's the greatest district. Finer people you won't meet.'
'Ack, da,' said the wee buck, 'all I see's a dirty street.'

Campbell worked in the Belfast docks from the 1950s until 1985. He has also been a senior trades union shop steward, and a member of the staff of Queen's University, Belfast. His most recent publications include Corner Kingdom, *a novel about Sailorstown, as well as a miscellany of writings about the district called* Once There Was a Community Here. *The verse portrait below of the bond between a hard-working man and his cat comes from his much-loved collection,* The Rose and the Blade: New and Selected Poems 1957–1997. *It was written in 1966.*

FACELESS MAGEE

I

We sat, one day, my cat and me.
My cat, by the way is called Faceless Magee.
Whilst slightly imbibed and feeling quite free,
we started talking, oul Faceless and me.
Don't get me wrong. As you will see,
the talking all was done by me.

II

Bathtubs, boats, peas and pods ...
I pause and smile as Faceless nods.
I said when cats roamed far Cathay
they hunted vermin every day.
Magee's black face lights as I talk.
He humps his back and starts to stalk.

I'm sure he'd keep the rats at bay
if he was out in far Cathay.
Magee and me had quite a chat,
he's pretty smart to be a cat.
His eyes shone wisdom, plain to see
he knows his onions, does Magee.

I told him 'bout the dog next door.
He spat and pranced about the floor
and flexed his paws as if to say
'I'd fight the canine any day.'
He rolled a little to the fire
and seemed quite ready to retire.

And so ended the tête à tee
that occurred last week
between Faceless and me.

Thomas Carnduff

*After his return from the Great War, Thomas Carnduff (1886–1956) joined
the standing army of Belfast ship-builders. A leading Independent Orange-
man, in 1924 he published* Songs from the Shipyard, *a first book of pol-
ished verses about working-class life.*

*His romantically muscular poems are sometimes, like the one below,
reminiscent of the best work of John Masefield, England's Poet Laureate at
the time. It appeared in his 1932 collection,* Songs of an Out-of-Work. *The
book's title tells its own story, alas: despite having his plays staged by the
Ulster Literary Theatre and the Abbey Theatre in Dublin, Carnduff was to
spend years working as a binman and in Civil Defence. Late in life he landed
a more congenial job as a caretaker in Belfast's Linenhall Library.*

ON THE NIGHT-SHIFT

God! But I'm sick of the launchways,
    And the lifelong creak of the crane,
The hiss of the scorching rivet,
    The twist of the iron frame,
The clang of a hundred hammers,
    The crooning hum of the drill,
The reckless swing of the staging
    That hurts with a sickly thrill—
The crash of the falling debris
    That holds your heart-beats still.

A weary week on the night-shift
    And I'm eating my grub in the dark,
Out on the deck, the upper deck,
    Where the night palls gloomy and stark;
With the star-dew flecking the bulwarks,
    An East wind whispering by
Like the voice of a woman fretting
    Or the wail of an infant's cry;—
Then the hush of a weird silence,
    And my heart speaks out in a sigh.

There's a strange, grim hush on the wavelets,
       A silent stealth in their stride
As they slip, uncanny and ghoulish,
       Close up to the liner's side.
A lone bird cries from the marshlands,
       A starlight beams in the sky,
Out on the lough where the sea-mew sleeps
       A spectral ship goes by—
And lo! We are in communion,
       Three lonely souls and I.

The gruff, harsh tones of my comrades
       Come up from the deck below,
Where the 'boys' of the card-school gather
       And the bulk of their spare cash go.
There's a vacant seat in the circle,
       A 'hand' dealt less on the right;
I can see my mate as he grumbles
       And swears in the candle-light—
But how could he know I was playing
       A lone 'hand' out in the night.

I shall go right down to the card-school,
       I shall plunge my all on an 'ace';
                    My mate shall shout me a welcome,
                         I shall laugh in the 'dealer's' face—

But out in the night a lone bird
    Will cry in the marshlands drear,
And out on the lough the port-lights
    Of a ghost-ship disappear,
And up in the sky a starlight
    Will fade like a passing tear.

Anonymous

The verses below come from one of the world's oldest 'rag mags'. A jewel in the crown of Queen's University, Belfast, Pro Tanto Quid *was founded in 1927 to raise money for local charities: it is still going strong. In the 1930s, like its contemporaries* Razzle *in London and Flann O'Brien's* Blather *in Dublin, the magazine was irreverent and decidedly risqué, featuring silhouettes of apparently naked maidens on tropical islands and cartoons of cocottes* en déshabillé. *It is still testing the limits of acceptability today.*

    The death of W.B. Yeats at the beginning of 1939 did not stop Pro Tanto Quid *from parodying his most famous poem in its issue of that year. These verses chillingly embody the sense of foreboding felt in Belfast as World War II began.*

THE WIND THAT DOES BE UP

I will arise and go now, and go to Innisfree,
And a small cabin build there, of steel and concrete made,
Nine gas-masks will I have there, and water H. and C.,
And live alone in the b—— air-raid.

I will arise and go now, for always night and day
I hear dictators yapping with low demands for more.
While I listen to Hitler, and Mussolini's bray
I get the wind up daily more and more.

Grizel Christie

A rare taste of the exotic from QUB. The couplets were inspired by a flamboyant set of murals that once adorned the backyard of the university's great anatomist Dr James Scott – who will appear as a poet himself later in this book. These lines appeared in The Northman *in autumn 1945; despite that journal's exclusivist title, they were written by a woman.*

The jungle of Jhong was tense and aware
And creepers writhed round the Tiger's lair.
By sinister fronds the Tiger lurked;
With sinister teeth the Tiger smirked.
The Bhapfish swam in the pool below,
Smiling a smile that was soft and slow
And thinking long thoughts of primeval slime
Where Bhapfish swim till the end of time.
The watching Tiger saw in the gloom
A sombre shadow betokening doom.

The Little Red Bird with the mocking whoop
Danced on the tip of a Flowering Choop.
(The flowers had fallen, the flowers were gone,
For the Choop-flower fades at the light of dawn.)
He stretched his leg and twirled it round
And sang a song that was most profound,
But no one could understand the words.
(That is the trouble with Little Red Birds.)
And the west wind blew his resonant song
Through the humid depths of the jungle of Jhong.

The man at the Mission opened his box
And planted a row of hollyhocks;
But the Savage destroyed the garden-plot
And boiled the Parson in his pot.
'Hubble bubble!' the Savage said.
'Cauldron bubble. Macbeth is dead.'
(For the Savage had taken a pass B.A.
And had read that highly instructive play.)
But the Parson alternately sank and floated
Which seemed to bear out the section quoted.

The Elephant breathed on the silent pool
And waved his trunk in the air to cool.
The heat of the jungle had turned him red
And dried the brains of his torpid head.
The Bhapfish gleamed in the yellow mud
With tail like amber and fins like blood
And scales like the jewels of Samarcand.
The dull-eyed Elephant saw and planned
And drank the pool and crushed the reeds.
(The Bhapfish was swallowed among the weeds.)

The Tiger's eyes were heavy with guile
And madness shone in his constant smile.
The twitching creepers recoiled in hate,
And the pool oozed back like sullen fate,
And the Tiger snarled with a cruel lust.
Blood dried on the creepers like crawling rust.
The Red Bird sang to the evening sky.
The Elephant listened with lazy eye.
The hidden evil is always strong
And the Tiger is lord in the jungle of Jhong.

John Clifford

Like many of the weaver poets and their poetic heirs, John Clifford (1900–83)
of Dickeystown, Glenarm, Co. Antrim, used words and spellings from Ulster-
Scots – the dialect recently christened 'Ullans'. Here he gives the reader a
vivid glimpse of the unregarded art of winnowing corn by hand to provide
winter feed for the animals. Probably written in the 1950s, the verses are taken
from the posthumous Poems of John Clifford, *edited by E. Logan for the*
Larne and District Folklore Society.

WULLIE BOYD'S FLAIL

When winter firmly tak's a houl',
An' days are dreary, drab an' coul',
Wi' bitter sleet an' drivin' hail,
Then Wullie Boyd tak's up his flail.

There's growin' stirks an' milkin' kye   *bullocks*
That needs fresh fother by and by,
So Wullie's flail gets intae gear
An' flings its echo far and near.

You'll hear him in the early morn,
Wi' steady thud he flails the corn,
He sees his beasts an' horses fed
Afore his neighbours lea' their bed.

I've often watched wi' boyish glee
How Wullie made the barley flee.
I've heard the aged rafters croak
Beneath his steady, measured stroke.

See how the neat begirdled sheaf
Sae pink o' stem, wi' glossy leaf,
Succumbs tae Wullie's practised skill—
A sturdy human threshin' mill.

A swish, a thud, the flail descends,
The tortured sheaf in agony bends;
The seed is scattered roun' like hail
'Neath Wullie's unrepentant flail.

Doon in the byre the drowsy kye
Are lyin' warm and snug and dry;
Unmindfu' o' the steady thud
They doze content, or chew the cud.

At last the flail is cast aside,
The wooden hatch is opened wide,
The eager beasts soon understan'
That breakfast time is noo at han'.

And Wullie sees each gets its share,
A liberal feed, wi' some tae spare;
An' then the kitchen's temptin' smell
Invites him forth tae feed himsel'.

There's two big rashers, side by side,
A blue duck egg in gravy fried,
An' fadge that tae your innards cling –   *potato-bread*
A breakfast fit for ony King.

Thus fortified, nae man can fail
Tae match the torture o' the flail,
For only sinews made o' steel
Can swing a flail – an' swing it weel.

There's something noble, grand and rare
Tae see a flail swish through the air;
There's mystic music in each stroke
As though some tribal drum had spoke.

So nivermore will I complain
If through my bedroom window-pane
The thud o' Wullie's flail should seep
An' spoil my early mornin' sleep.

Instead, I'll maybe breathe a prayer,
And think o' Wullie toilin' there,
But nivermore I'll be annoyed
Tae hear the flail o' Wullie Boyd!

Anonymous

This eccentric shaggy dog story from Co. Antrim is another discovery from Richard Hayward's Ulster Songs and Ballads of the Town and the Country. *'Crebilly' Fair, as it was pronounced, received its Charter from King Charles I; a legendary magnet for beggars, it was still held there annually until relatively recently.*

CRAIGBILLY FAIR

As I went up to Craigbilly Fair,
Who did I meet but a jolly beggar,
And the name of this beggar they callèd him Rover,
And the name of his wife it was Kitty-lie-over;
There was Rover and Rover and Kitty-lie-over,
There was Rooney and Mooney,
And Nancy and Francey,
And Lily and Billy,
And Jamie and Joe;
And away went the beggar-men all in a row.

Again I went up to Craigbilly Fair,
And who should I meet but another beggar,
And this beggar's name they callèd him Rallax,
And the name of his wife it was Ould Madam Ball-o'-Wax;
There was Rallax and Rallax and Ould Madam Ball-o'-Wax,
There was Rover and Rover and Kitty-lie-over,
There was Rooney and Mooney,
And Nancy and Francey,
And Lily and Billy,
And Jamie and Joe;
And away went the beggar-men all in a row.

Again I went up to Craigbilly Fair,
And who should I meet but another beggar,
And the name of this beggar they callèd him Dick,
And the name of his wife it was Ould Lady Splooter-stick;
There was Dick and Dick and Ould Lady Splooter-stick,
There was Rallax and Rallax and ould Madam Ball-o'-Wax,
There was Rover and Rover and Kitty-lie-over,
There was Rooney and Mooney,
And Nancy and Francey,
And Lily and Billy,
And Jamie and Joe;
And away went the beggar-men all in a row.

John Dickey

John Dickey was born in Belfast as the eighteenth century was drawing to a close. He was yet another weaving poet, as he explains:

> *And for my trade I'm by the by*
> *A lazy-greasy weaver.*

> I'll ne'er despise the weaving trade,
> The shuttle's lighter than the spade,
> But if I have a living made
>   This mony a day
> There's some high nebs, if it should fade
>   Would soon look blae.

In 1812 Dickey wrote to introduce himself to James Orr, one of the most eminent of the rhyming weavers. Compared to Orr he was, he said, just a 'rhyming blockhead blether'. Dickey's youthful sense of low self-esteem did not last: six years later he brought out his own volume of verse, dubiously honouring his mentor by giving it the same inspiring title that Orr had chosen for his own collection: Poems on Various Subjects.

BE THIS MY LOT

A cow and a pig, and a bonny bit land,
A trifle of money still at my command,
To live independent, – I love to be free,
A competent portion is plenty for me.

I never will scramble to heap up a store,
For heir's wide to scatter when I am no more;
Nor yet will I squander what heaven has lent,
But plenish my cabin, and pay up the rent.

And when I'm a husband, may I have
      a wife
   Who'll make it her study to sweeten
      my life,
   And love to be thrifty, and careful of all,
     That things may be decent when
        visitors call.

Lynn C. Doyle

These days, the best-known literary creation of Lynn C. Doyle (1873–1961) may be his clever pseudonym. Born Leslie A. Montgomery in Co. Down, he had a 'proper' career as a banker, rising to manager of a branch in Dundalk. He also wrote plays, verses and other works, winning his greatest success with the Ballygullion series, which was issued in periodic volumes over almost forty years. Some commentators have found these comic chronicles of life in a fictional parish in Co. Armagh to be embarrassingly stage-Irish, but Doyle's writing had undeniable charm, and he had a good ear for the speech of rural Ulster – as he amply demonstrates in the poem below.

THE DISCOVERY

I was comin' from the ploughin'
One evenin' in October,
My boots were full of clabber   *mud*
An' my coat was dreepin' rain,   *dripping*
My feet were like two lumps of ice,
My fingers clubbed like carrots,
An' my back was like a rusted hinge
With rheumatism pain.
But when I reached the kitchen
An' saw a wheen of neighbours,   *several*
An' glasses, jugs, an' muddlers,   *stirrers*
I knowed I wouldn't die;
An' till this day I can't forget
The shout our Mick let out of him:
'I've found a keg of poteen in the wee pig's sty!'

My blessin' on the decent chap
That mixed the wash an' used the worm,

On the man that scobed the barrel,   *scoured out*
An' him that hooped it round;
A blessin' on the rootin' nose
That hoked the earth away from it,   *dug*
An' pardon for the Peelers
That made it go to ground.
For care an' toil are only whets   *incitements*
To help us how to play ourselves,
An' love is better far nor drink,
An' drink than goin' dry;
An' love an' fun an' kindliness
Descended on our dwellin'-place
The night we found the poteen in the wee pig's sty.

Although I'd missed two rounds of punch
I very soon made up on them,
My toes were tinglin' quicksilver,
That had been stuck with glar,   *mud*
My farm was all the universe,
With divil an annuity,
I was harrowin' the heavens
With a comet an' a star.
Ezekiel M'Intaggart
That morning was a Methodist,
That night he was a pooka,
An' oul' limpin' Pat Mackye
Was prancin' round our slavey   *maid*
With his club-foot, an' sciatica,
The night we found the poteen in the wee pig's sty.

Young Peter Gurt had sighed for years
For little Rosie Gormaghan,
And must have found his bravery
In barley an' the moon.

That night he popped the question,
Without any ambiguity,
He married her in April,
An' the child was born in June.
I know it's bad morality,
But blame it on the Government,
For them that can't get houses
Must court beneath the sky,
An' if I'm not a deal mistook
They sowed a grain of shamrock-seed
The night we found the poteen in the wee pig's sty.

Percy French

Though Percy French (1854–1920) was not an Ulsterman, he almost was, for he went to school in Foyle College, Co. Derry, and later served time in Cavan as a drain-inspector. He was there in 1883 when the volcano Krakatoa (west of Java) erupted: the watercolours he painted of the consequent spectacular sunsets launched him on a lucrative sideline career as an artist. After the world of drains had dispensed with his services, in 1891 French took to his bicycle, pedalling around Ireland with his banjo and his painting kit, and whenever he reached a town he presented a one-man show to display his many talents.

One day in 1896, on top of the Hill of Howth in Co. Dublin, French noticed the outline of the Mourne Mountains, far to the north in Co. Down. He jotted some lines onto a postcard and sent them to his collaborator, the 'musical humorist' Dr W. Houston Collison, who set them to music. Written in the already familiar form of a letter home from an innocent Irishman abroad, the song became one of Percy French's most famous. The lyrics are well worth revisiting on the page, since in performance their gentle humour is perhaps overshadowed by the particularly lovely tune.

Oh, Mary, this London's a wonderful sight,
Wid the people here workin' by day and by night;
    They don't sow potatoes, nor barley, nor wheat,
    But there's gangs o' them diggin' for gold in the street—
At least, when I axed them, that's what I was told,
So I just took a hand at this diggin' for gold,
    But for all that I found there, I might as well be
    Where the Mountains o' Mourne sweep down to the sea.

I believe that, when writin', a wish you expressed
As to how the fine ladies in London were dressed.
    Well, if you'll believe me, when axed to a ball,
    They don't wear a top to their dresses at all!
Oh, I've seen them meself, and you could not, in trath,
Say if they were bound for a ball or a bath—
    Don't be startin' them fashions now, Mary Machree,
    Where the Mountains o' Mourne sweep down to the sea.

I seen England's King from the top of a 'bus—
I never knew him, though he means to know us:
    And though by the Saxon we once were oppressed,
    Still, I cheered – God forgive me – I cheered wid the rest.
And now that he's visited Erin's green shore,
We'll be much better friends than we've been heretofore,
    When we've got all we want, we're as quiet as can be
    Where the Mountains o' Mourne sweep down to the sea.

You remember young Peter O'Loughlin, of course—
Well, here he is now at the head o' the Force.
    I met him to-day, I was crossin' the Strand,
    And he stopped the whole street wid wan wave of his hand:

And there we stood talking of days that are gone,
While the whole population of London looked on;
    But for all these great powers, he's wishful like me,
    To be back where the dark Mourne sweeps down to the sea.

There's beautiful girls here – oh! never mind!
With beautiful shapes Nature never designed,
    And lovely complexions, all roses and crame,
    But O'Loughlin remarked wid regard to the same:
'That if at those roses you venture to sip,
The colour might all come away on your lip,'
    So I'll wait for the wild rose that's waitin' for me—
    Where the Mountains o' Mourne sweep down to the sea.

John Gallen

This most peculiar wedding ode was published in the Northman *in the autumn of 1941; it is intriguing to wonder what 'K.F.', to whom it is dedicated, can have made of it. John Gallen was then joint editor with Robert Greacen of the* QUB *magazine, which they were trying to turn into 'the literary voice of Ulster'. For a while they almost succeeded – largely because there were no other contenders for the title. Greacen would go on to have a productive literary career, dying as recently as 2008, but in January 1947 Gallen's death on active service in the mountains of India with the Royal Irish Fusiliers cut short a writing life of unusual and unpredictable promise.*

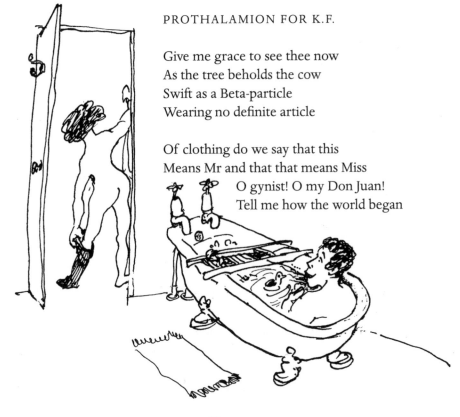

PROTHALAMION FOR K.F.

Give me grace to see thee now
As the tree beholds the cow
Swift as a Beta-particle
Wearing no definite article

Of clothing do we say that this
Means Mr and that that means Miss
O gynist! O my Don Juan!
Tell me how the world began

Embracing is an awful habit
E.g. the house-fly and the rabbit
Selon the moralists are horrid
But I behind my pensive forehead

Find them intrinsically funny
As, I have no doubt, does the bunny

Solomon in all his glory
Was not arrayed like one of these
Monogamists on bended knees
But that is quite another story.

(Moral: There are occasions which call for ambiguity.)

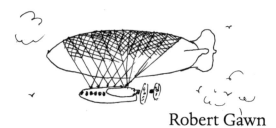

Robert Gawn

'Nineteen and Sixty' was found among a collection of handwritten poems,
songs and recitations belonging to the late Mat Meharg, of Ballyboley, Co.
Antrim, which his sister has kindly allowed us to examine. An accompany-
ing note states that the verses were written in 1926: clearly the author had a
pretty good idea of what lay in store for the world.

NINETEEN AND SIXTY

Away in the days when our fathers were young
Our trousers were made of good-wearing homespun,
Our coats made for comfort, to keep out the cold,
Our boots made of leather, not tinsel and gold.

But sure I forget those days are gone by
And the age that we live in, between you and I,
Is flying so fast it would take a balloon
To keep up with its pace over country and town.

Just a hundred years back, farmers' carts they were made
For to take out manure and bring peats from the glade,
But now they have motors fast driven by oil:
No labours for horses, for mankind no toil.

Sure the folks they're all changed, you would scarcely believe—
Women's skirts to their knees, in their bodice no sleeve,
Their hair is cut short, just the same as a man
So they look a facsimile of Peter or Tam.

You can sit in your parlour and watch picture plays,
Or converse with the spirits of forgotten old days
And the clergy that preach make it clear there's no hell,
But assure one and all that in heaven they'll dwell.

Padric Gregory

Although he was given a long entry in the 1923 Thom's Irish Who's Who, *the Belfast poet and folklorist Padric Gregory (1886–1962) does not appear at all in most recent reference books – not even in the* Oxford Companion to Irish Literature. *Presumably this is because his work is no longer considered to be 'literature'. An architect by profession – he designed the Roman Catholic Cathedral in Johannesburg – he was an avid collector of what he called 'old peasant songs and tunes', and many of his own verses were set to music. A note in his book* Ulster Songs and Ballads *(1920) states – and it seems surprising – that 'The Ninepenny Pig' was based on 'old folksong fragments'. Be that as it may, the verses have a certain indefinable charm.*

THE NINEPENNY PIG

My father an' mother were Irish,
An' I am Irish, too;
They bought a wee pig for nine-pence,
An' it was Irish, too;
But it wudnae grow a big pig,
An' Da took it away
Tae Lisnalinchey Market,
All on a Market day.

An' whin he took the crathur
Away from us I sighed,
It knowed, itself, 'twas goin'
For oh, it squealed an' cried,
But ivery time I'd coax Da
Tae keep it, he'd say: 'No!
The fairy-folk hae charmed it,
An' it'll niver grow.'

It strunted, an' it grunted,   *sulked*
But Da driv it away,
Tae Lisnalinchey Market,
All on a market day;
An' up there comes a show-man—
Who'd come for the May Fair—
An' says he, tae Da, says he: 'Sir,
What is it ye hae there?'

An' Da says tae the show-man:
'I'm sellin' this wee pig,
For, though I've stuffed an' fed it,
The crowl'll nae grow big.'   *runt*
They bargained an' they haggled,
They argued up an' down,
An' then at last Da sould it—
All for a silver crown.

The show-man took that pigeen
An' larnt it tricks, for weeks;
He dhressed it in a waistcoat,
An' swallow-tailed, an' breeks;   *coat*
He larnt it for till stand up,
An' walk, an' sit, an' kneel,
An' rowll aboot, an' tumble,
An' dance an Irish reel.

An' now, folk say, that show-man
Has goold an' goold galore;
And that he does nae thravel
On Fair-days ony more:
He's marrit tae some ladie
O' great an' high degree,

43

All through the pig he bought from
My foolish Da an' me.

My father an' mother were Irish,
An' I am Irish, too;
They bought a wee pig for nine-pence,
An' it was Irish, too;
But it wudnae grow a big pig,
An' Da took it away
Tae Lisnalinchey Market,
All on a Market day.

Albert Haslett

*Albert Haslett is a well-known Belfast poet and local historian. Born in
1926, he grew up in a family of ten children in the Shankill Road area of
Belfast. For some years he led 'Shankill Safaris', sharing his lively memories
of a time when the district had over 50,000 more residents than today, and
describing the devastation wreaked by the Luftwaffe during the early years
of World War II.*

*This delightful anecdote in verse comes from a small book of his poems,
entitled* Enjoy the Crack!

HOLY WATER

A nun was driving in her car, when she ran out of gas,
So she walked back to a station that she had only passed.
She said 'I need some petrol, but I haven't got a tin.
Could you lend me anything at all that I could put it in?'

The man looked round about the shop, he even tried the store,
He searched about the yard as well, and behind the toilet door;
At last he said, 'I'm sorry dear,' then he whispered low,
'The only thing I have in here is this old fashioned po.'

The nun she said, 'Sure that's alright, the car's not far away,
If you don't mind I'll use it, and bring it back another day.'
So he held the po beneath the pump, filled it up with good four star;
The nun she thanked him very much and walked back to the car.

A gallon was what the po just held, filled right to the top;
She walked back very slowly, and never spilt a drop,
Got a funnel from the boot, pushed back a straying hair—
As she started pouring petrol in, she said a silent prayer.

Now this wee man came on the scene, walking along the bank,
He saw this nun with po held high, pouring stuff into the tank,
He walked right up beside the nun, and said with bated breath,
'I don't have your religion, but I wish I had your faith.'

Crawford Howard

Great Verse to Stand Up and Tell Them, edited by Doreen McBride, was published in 1996 by the Adare Press, Banbridge. An excellent anthology of Northern Irish poems intended to be read out loud, it contains several contributions from Crawford Howard, Belfast poet and entertainer extraordinaire. This is one of them – in which he gives a few unusual twists to those familiar old snakes that St Patrick sent into exile.

ST PATRICK AND THE SNAKES

You've heard of the snakes in Australia,
  You've heard of the snakes in Japan,
   You've heard of the rattler – that old Texas battler—
     Whose bite can mean death to a man.
         They've even got snakes in old England—
Nasty adders all yellow and black—
But in Erin's green isle we can say with a smile
They're away – and they're not coming back!

Now years ago things was quite different—
There was serpents all over the place.
If ye climbed up a ladder ye might meet an adder,
Or a cobra might lep at your face,
If ye went for a walk up the Shankill,
Or a dander along Sandy Row,
A flamin' great python would likely come within'
An' take a lump outa yer toe!

Now there once was a guy called St Patrick,
A preacher of fame and renown—
An' he hoisted his sails and came over from Wales
To convert all the heathens in Down,

An' he hirpled about through the country   *hobbled*
With a stick an' a big pointy hat,
An' he kept a few sheep that he sold on the cheap,
But sure there's no money in that!

He was preachin' a sermon in Comber
An gettin' quite carried away
An' he mentioned that Rome had once been his home
(But that was the wrong thing to say!)
For he felt a sharp pain in his cheek-bone
An' he stuck up a hand till his bake   *mouth*
An' the thing that had lit on his gub (an' had bit)   *mouth*
Was a wee Presbyterian snake!

Now the snake slithered down from the pulpit
(Expectin' St Patrick to die),
But yer man was no dozer – he lifted his crozier
An' he belted the snake in the eye,
And he says till the snake, 'Listen legless!
You'd just better take yerself aff!
If you think that that trick will work with St Patrick
You must be far worser nor daft!'

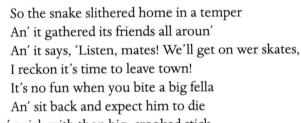

So the snake slithered home in a temper
An' it gathered its friends all aroun'
An' it says, 'Listen, mates! We'll get on wer skates,
I reckon it's time to leave town!
It's no fun when you bite a big fella
An' sit back and expect him to die
An' he's so flamin' quick with thon big, crooked stick
That he hits ye a dig in the eye!'

48

So a strange sight confronted St. Patrick
When he woke up the very next day.
The snakes with long faces were all packin' their cases
An' headin' for Donegall Quay.
Some got on cheap flights to Majorca
And some booked apartments in Spain.
They were all headin' out and there wasn't a doubt
That they weren't going to come back again.

So the reason the snakes left old Ireland,
(An' this is no word of a lie),
They all went to places to bite people's faces
And be reasonably sure that they'd die.
An' the oul' snakes still caution their grandsons,
'For God's sake beware of St Pat!
An' take yerselves aff if you see his big staff,
An' his cloak, an' his big pointy hat!'

'The Diagonal Steel Trap' is probably Crawford Howard's most celebrated work. As a student, he occasionally went with friends to Harland and Wolff's on Queen's Island in the mouth of the River Lagan, and did a day's unpaid labour there, unnoticed by any of the 'hats' (as the bowler-hatted foremen were called). By then, the aircraft factory section of the Belfast firm had been destroyed by an air-raid in 1941, but the shipyard was still thriving, and so the young volunteer was able to pick up the lore that he would later put to such good use in this epic 'recitation'.

THE DIAGONAL STEEL TRAP

Now they built a big ship down in Harland's
She was made for to sell to the Turks,
And they called on the Yard's chief designer
To design all the engines and works.

Now finally the engines was ready
And they screwed in the very last part,
An' yer man says 'Let's see how she runs, lads!'
An' bejesus! The thing wouldn't start.

So they pushed and they worked an' they footered,
An' the engineers' faces got red,
The designer he stood lookin' stupid,
An' scratchin' the back o' his head.

But while they were fiddlin' and workin',
Up danders oul' Jimmie Dalzell,
He had worked twenty years in the 'Island'
And ten in the 'aircraft' as well.

So he pushed and he worked and he muttered,
Till he got himself through till the front,

And he had a good look roun' the engine,
An' he gives a few mutters and grunts.

And then he looks up at the gaffer,
An' says he, 'Mr Smyth, d'ye know?
They've left out the Diagonal Steam Trap!
How the hell d'ye think it could go?'

Now the engineer eyed the designer
The designer he looks at the 'hat',
And they whispered the one to the other,
'Diagonal Steam Trap? What's that?'

But the Gaffer, he wouldn't admit, like
To not knowin' what this was about,
So he says 'Right enough, we were stupid!
The Diagonal Steam Trap's left out!'

Now in the meantime oul' Jimmie had scarpered,
Away down to throw in his boord,
And the Gaffer comes up and says 'Jimmy!
D'ye think we could have a wee word?

Ye see that Diagonal Steam Trap?
I know it's left out – that's bad luck,
But the engine shop's terrible busy,
D'ye think ye could knock us one up?'

Now, oul' Jimmy was laughin' his scone off
He had made it all up for a gag,
He seen what was stoppin' the engine—
The feed-pipe was blocked with a rag!

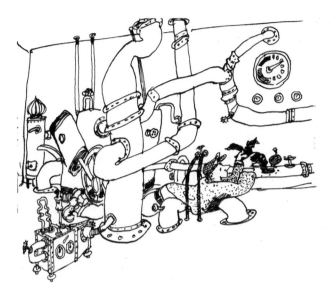

But he sticks the oul' hands in the pockets,
An' he says 'Aye, I'll give yez a han'!
I'll knock yez one up in the mornin',
An' the whole bloody thing will be grand!'

So oul' Jimmy starts to work the next mornin',
To make what he called a Steam Trap,
An oul' box an' a few bits of tubing,
An' a steam gauge stuck up on the top.

An' he welds it all on till the engine,
An' he says to the wonderin' mob,
'As long as that gauge is at zero,
The Steam Trap is doin' its job!'

Then he pulls the rag outa the feed-pipe,
An' he gives the oul' engine a try,
An' bejesus, she goes like the clappers,
An' oul' Jimmy remarks, 'That's her nye!'

Now the ship was the fastest seen ever,
So they sent her away till the Turks,
But they toul' them, 'That Steam Trap's a secret!
We're the only ones knows how it works!'

But the Turks they could not keep their mouths shut,
An' soon the whole story got roun',
An' the Russians got quite interested—
Them boys has their ears to the groun'!

So they sent a spy dressed as a sailor,
To take photies of Jimmy's Steam Trap,
An' they got them all back till the Kremlin,
An' they stood round to look at the snaps.

Then the head spy says, 'Mr Kosygin!
I'm damned if I see how that works!'
So they sent him straight off to Siberia,
An' they bought the whole ship from the Turks!

When they found the Steam Trap was a 'cod' like,
They couldn't admit they'd been had,
So they built a big factory in Moscow,
To start makin' Steam Traps like mad!

Then Mr Kosygin rings up Mr Nixon
And says, 'Youse'uns thinks yez are great!
But wi' our big new Russian made Steam Trap,
Yez'll find that we've got yez all bate!'

Now oul' Nixon, he nearly went 'Harpic',
So he thought he'd give Harland's a call,
So he dialled the engine-shop number,
And of course he got sweet bugger all!

54

But at last the call came through to Jimmy,
In the midst of a terrible rush,
'There's a call for you from the White House!'
Says oul' Jim, 'That's a shop in Portrush!'

There's a factory outside of Seattle,
Where they're turnin' out Steam Traps like hell,
It employs twenty-five thousand workers,
And the head of it—
            Jimmy Dalzell!

Anonymous

A charming jeu d'esprit *about the conciliatory effects of sharing good food and drink. It was written in 1935 for the Queens' rag-mag,* Pro Tanto Quid.

IN VINO VERITAS

The cakes I ate,
Begob, were great,
The wine, by me sowl, was mellow.
I dreamt the town
O' Portydown
Was painted green and yellow;
And Newry, too,
Red, white and blue,
And fifes to drums were squealing,
And Billy went home
Wi' the Pope o' Rome
To show there was no ill feeling.

John Jarvis

The greatest natural sportsmen ever to come out of Ulster were probably George Best and Alex 'Hurricane' Higgins. When either of them played, audiences knew that almost anything could happen. John Jarvis (b. 1917) here brilliantly captures the mounting tension and excitement that Higgins has always caused around the snooker table – and indeed everywhere else he goes.

THE HURRICANE

The chattering dies as the players walk in,
A handshake, a nod, and a smile.
Partisan feeling is almost a sin
Earth stops in its course for a while.

The table is true and the cloth is as green
As pasture on Mid-Summer Day.
Where have they come from and what have they seen,
These giants who step out to play?

The opening frame, Alex Higgins to break,
These words have hardly been said,
Than Alex is up with the speed of a snake,
Kissed the blue and gone in off a red.

His opponent is careful and seizes his chance,
With some fine methodical play.
A push here, a nudge there and sometimes a glance,
His victory's well on its way.

He pots several blacks, an occasional pink,
Higgins' eyes have followed each shot,
Between smoking and puffing and taking a drink
He's wondering what chances he's got.

His opponent finally runs out of steam,
He's already scored fifty-eight
His victory is now much more than a dream
Higgins must swallow his fate.

Alex comes to the table with no sign of fear,
He knows just what he must do.
He can't get a red and the black is well clear,
So he snookers behind the blue.

His opponent is peering, but can't see the red,
He's been sipping his water, or gin,
Alex's snooker has left him for dead,
He doesn't know where to begin.

He misses and Alex pops up like a cork,
He's already striking the white.
He's just heard he's had a big winner at York,
It could be one hell of a night!

He puts down five reds, three blacks and a brown
He's now got his sights on the blue.
If he gets it, they'll hear it way down in the town,
In Belfast and Manchester too.

Like a crack from a gun it flies into the sack,
There's only the colours to go.
One after another right down to the black,
They fall to each hurricane blow.

Snooker's played on 'the green', and it pays to be bold,
Each click of the balls sounds like cricket.
The crowd rise as they did to the Bradman of old,
When Hurricane 'comes to the wicket'.

Paul Jennings

The English columnist and humorist Paul Jennings (1943–89) was a teenager when he wrote 'Ballyburbling'. The lines owe their origin to the Northern Ireland Telephone Directory, in which Jennings noticed that the address of one subscriber was 'Ballymackleduff, Derryfubble, Benburb'. The Observer *published the verses in July 1959, and six years later Colm Ó Lochlainn welcomed them into the Irish canon by including them in his book,* More Irish Street Ballads.

BALLYBURBLING

Och, the world was full of grievin', an' when I'd had enough
I packed me bag and set me face towards Ballymackleduff;
White houses nestle there, all far from toil an' trouble
Ah the lough an' the sea-birds an' sweet Derryfubble!
I thought me heart would melt for joy, an' nothin' might disturb
The peace that I'd be findin' in beautiful Benburb.

O! the friends of me youth was
    there to make me comin' merry,
First I drank with Mick the Tanner
    just a mile from Fubblederry
An' Roarin' Pat was waitin' in the
    bar at Mackleben
'Begod,' says he, 'have one with
    me'; three jolly Irish men
With all the pints o' porter, the
    gossip an' the cackle
'Twas dancin' in the road we was
    that goes to Derrymackle.

Then up spake Mick the Tanner that was born in Fubblemack
'The boys at Ballyfubble will be glad to see ye back—
Let's be goin' to O'Reilly's, where the Fiddler of Benbally
An' the Fubblederry Fluter is in his Dancin' Palais
An' the girls from Ferrymackle, an' from Bubblefurbyduff
Is doin' all the jiggin' an' the rock-an'-rollin' stuff.'

Ah, hadn't we the time at all at Glubbymacklederry
With all the folk from Grabble an' from Ballygubbleferry
An' Mackledubblegurgle, an' Blubberderryglen
An' the lasses from Duffmackle, an' the rantin' Burble men,
The Squintin' Men from Brackle, an' Mrs Tom MacNally
An' the seven black-haired sisters that live over in Duffbally.

An' wilder came the music from the Fubblederry Flute
An' Mick was drinking Guinness from the Widow Leary's boot
An' Roarin' Pat was fightin' with a man from Derryburble
That laid him out and wrote a sign that said DO NOT DISTURBLE.
O! shut was all the factories, and open all the bars,
There was laughter in the lamplight and kissin' by the stars,
Delight in Derryfubble; and Benburb was full of song;
Ah, Ballymackleduff! Why *did* I stay away so long?

Anonymous

This 'jingle', as it calls itself, appeared in the summer of 1940 in the New Northman, *bearing the (so far) unidentified initials, 'E.E.S.' It is doubtless fanciful to draw links to the bardic 'dinnshenchas' tradition of Gaelic topographical verse, but these unassuming lines, with their vivid bird's-eye view of north-east Co. Derry, lend a strikingly sensuous quality to the landscape. Several other pieces in the magazine by the same writer are equally driven by thwarted sexual urges – but then the top of a hill isn't usually the best place to seek a romantic encounter, or as it is called here, a 'coort'.*

JUNIPER HILL

I climbed to the summit of Juniper Hill
    To observe the grand view of the shore.
And indeed I could easily be standing there still
Without having finished observing my fill
    From Magilligan Point to Bengore,
    Though it's often I've seen it before.

When I turned to the right 'twas a beautiful sight
    To look down on the town of Portrush.
And I thought to myself that I very well might
Have the time to walk down there before it fell night
    To buy a new whitewashing brush
    Or a billhook to thin out a bush.

Then I looked to the left and below me as well
    Were the neat little streets of Portstewart.
And at once I remembered of having heard tell,
Though they might have no whitewashing brushes to sell,
    That the girls are all fond of a coort
    That reside in the town of Portstewart.

I thought of the lasses so lovely and gay
    And the notions ran round in my head.
Will I go to Portrush or the opposite way?
Will I squander my money on dancing and tay
    Or buy a new billhook instead,
    And go quietly home to my bed?

And while I was thinking the shadows grew long,
    And I turned on the heel of my fut
And went into Portstewart, and perhaps I was wrong
To go hunting for kisses and wenches and song
    When the house wanted whitewashing, but—
    Sure the shops would be sure to be shut.

Felix Kearney

These verses are something of a mystery. Found among Mat Meharg's collection, they were clearly marked 'Felix Kearney', but they can hardly have been written by the only poet of that name we have yet managed to identify. (That particular Felix Kearney was a gifted songwriter and musician, born in 1889 near Drumquin, Co. Tyrone. He left school at nine, became a farmer's boy at twelve, and after seeing service in World War I, worked for the rest of his life as a casual farm labourer. In about 1950 his Songs and Poems of Tyrone *was published, gentle verses in praise of local beauty spots.)*

By contrast, the gritty lines below describe the city of Belfast under attack during World War II, as the German Luftwaffe bombards all around the Harland and Wolff shipyard on its island in the Lagan. The narrator seems to have a staunchly loyalist perspective on the world, embracing the old Orange Lodge certainties of the 'Glorious Memory' of King Billy. But as the poem concludes, we are left wondering whether things are always quite as they appear.

THE BLITZ

My name is Sammy Thompson
And the place of my abode
Is the grandest place in Belfast,
The good old Shankill Road.
I stay in bed on Sunday
And leave the church to them it fits,
And I never tucked in with the Fenians
Till Hitler sent the Blitz.

I mind the night he came to us:
'Twas tough, I'm telling you,
I was down in Billy Johnston's pub
And had a pint or two.
We heard the siren going
And says Billy, 'Sam my son,
I think you should be blowing
If you want to see the fun.'

Don't think that I was breezy,
I was nothing of the kind.
I had often fought the Fenians—
I could beat the beggars blind,
So I stepped out right and manly
Till I heard an awful crack,
Then I made for home like blazes
And never once looked back.

The slates and glass were flying—
There were other things, you know,
That would mind you of the rivets
The Islandmen would throw.
I was fair done out with running,
At my heart I took a pain,
So I cursed the Pope in case
I wouldn't have the chance again.

I shouted 'No Surrender!'
I had not the slightest doubt
But that some among the Germans
Would recognise that shout.
But they never seemed to notice,
The bombs fell thick and fast;
I've a notion there were Fenians
In the lot that strafed Belfast.

When at last I reached the Shankill
I was in a proper funk.
I found the house deserted
And the wife had done a bunk.
I besought the Glorious Memory
In my misery and gloom
And remembered that the Lodge's flag
Was in the wee back room.

I had a job before me then—
In sowl it was no joke—
I would have to save the banner
Should Belfast go up in smoke;
So I grabbed it up and started out
To find a safer spot
When a brick or something hit me,
And I thought I had been shot.

I knew I would be safe
If I reached the Orange Hall
And that's where I was going
When I had this nasty fall.
When I regained my sense
The worst had come to pass—
I was in a Papish chapel
Where the Fenians go to Mass!

'Twas then I thought about my flag
And started looking round:
In a corner of the chapel
Was the colours safe and sound;
But a miracle had happened
For when daylight came I could see
The good old orange banner
Was streaked orange white and green.

I went and left the turncoat flag
Outside the Chapel walls;
I hear a Fenian lifted it
And took it to the Falls.
And when the Missus saw me
She had seven kinds of fits—
She had hoped she was a widow,
And was thankful for the Blitz.

John 'Paul' Kelly

A long admirer of Robbie Burns (arguably the presiding deity of Ulster's 'folk' poets), John 'Paul' Kelly (1884–1944) lived in Doon, a townland near Draperstown, Co. Derry, where his mother was the local schoolteacher. A book of his work, In Crockmore's Shade: Poems of John 'Paul' Kelly, *was compiled in 1991 by Graham Mawhinney, and it is from that collection that the following unsolicited advertisement for Millar's Jam is taken. The verses get along splendidly until the very last line, when they – dare one say it? – come to a rather sticky end.*

MILLAR'S JAM

History tells us some lengthened tales
Of man's achievement here,
With searchlights on the distant past
To make the days look clear.

When Eve betrayed the sacred trust
And pulled the apple down
Her comrade Adam knew the deed
And viewed her with a frown.

He cautioned her so shy at first,
Then with his open palm,
Said she 'The world must know and learn
Of Millar's Irish Jam.'

They started on that awful night,
Of terror and of rain,
When Ararat was reached at last
Two pots did but remain.

The Roman people built a name
Which on earth will never die,
Her eagle flew an endless space
O'er earth and azure sky.

The Roman Empire's mighty sway
Would stand the last exam,
Had all their soldiers streaked their bread
With Millar's Marvellous Jam.

Charlemagne encouraged art
And culture every way,
And while he lived his nation grew
And served him many a day.

He built a chest of cedar wood
For storing Eastern Balm,
But when he read the
labels there
It was Millar's Irish Jam.

It's here today the standard food
Of millions rich and poor.
It flourished in the early times
And made its home secure.

The navy says it's pleasantest,
The farmer says it's grand,
The coachmen says it's first of first,
In all of our known land.

The waitress says it's folly,
The head cook says the same,
To run a large refreshment room
And blot out Millar's name.

So the professor calls its virtues up,
The judge says 'Here I am,
The source of all our stamina
Is Millar's Irish Jam.'

The jellies and their high preserves,
The grand prix always get,
Their smoke stacks are
    a beacon light,
On Ravenhill, Belfast.

Jimmy Kennedy

No book of Ulster's Other Poetry could possibly leave out 'Teddy Bears Picnic'. It is probably the most famous thing ever to be written by anyone from the province. Jimmy Kennedy (1902–84) was born in Omagh, Co. Tyrone, and grew up among the trippers of Portstewart, Co. Londonderry. After university (at Trinity College Dublin), he began writing song lyrics, and in 1931 Gracie Fields gave him his first big success with 'The Barmaid's Song'. Extremely prolific, he went on to international glory with over two hundred other compositions, including 'Red Sails in the Sunset'. Indeed, until Lennon and McCartney, he is said to have had more hits in the United States than any non-American.

But Kennedy's most durable song is certainly 'Teddy Bears Picnic'. He wrote the lyrics to fit an already existing tune (composed in 1907 by J.W. Bratton), and the classic recording – the one we all still know – was issued in 1932 by Henry Hall and his Orchestra.

TEDDY BEARS PICNIC

If you go down in the woods today
You're sure of a big surprise
If you go down in the woods today
You'd better go in disguise

For ev'ry Bear that ever there was
Will gather there for certain, because
Today's the day the Teddy Bears have their picnic.

Picnic time for Teddy Bears,
The little Teddy Bears are having a lovely time today
Watch them, catch them unawares
And see them picnic on their holiday

See them gaily gad about,
They love to play and shout;
They never have any cares;
At six o'clock their Mummies and Daddies
    will take them home to bed
Because they're tired little Teddy Bears.

Ev'ry Teddy Bear who's been good
Is sure of a treat today
There's lots of marvellous things to eat,
And wonderful games to play

Beneath the trees where nobody sees
They'll hide and seek as long as they please
'Cause that's the way the Teddy Bears have their picnic.

(Repeat verse 3, then 1, 2, & 3)

70

Anonymous

During World War II in Belfast, as German bombs rained down, it was hard enough to keep cheerful, and even the advertisements did what they could to turn the situation to advantage. This one flirted with tastelessness when it appeared in Pro Tanto Quid *in 1941, accompanied by a cartoon showing an injured soldier in hospital.*

'KENNEDY'S BREAD'

He's lying in bed
But he would have been dead
If he hadn't been fed
On 'Kennedy's Bread'.

Mick McAtamney

Not so many years ago, Seamus Heaney wrote a forward to a little book entitled Honey to the Ear: The Poems of Liam McAllister and Mick McAtamney. *Published in Maghera, largely for local distribution, it gathered the best poems by two 'poets of the past' from south Derry. Although he doesn't explicitly say so, it is clear that Heaney's preference is for the less literary of the two, Mick McAtamney (1862–1946), who had a fresh, no-nonsense voice that was all his own – as can be seen in this stray verse from an early composition:*

> *I was born on a stormy morning*
> *In eighteen-sixty-two,*
> *The snow was flying and I was crying,*
> *There wasn't much else that I could do.*

McAtamney lived for a time in the United States, and evidently, if we believe the lines below, he had travelled extensively elsewhere as well. When he died in Derry, he left, it is said, 'only his poems' behind him.

THE IRISH FLEA

I got stung by yellow jacket
   And bit by hornet too,
      And eaten by mosquitoes
         In the swamp of Kalamazoo.

Pests of every quality
Are all well known to me
But for downright raciality
You take the Irish Flea.

Mickey MacConnell

Mickey MacConnell (b. 1947) is a native of Bellanaleck, near Enniskillen, Co. Fermanagh. At only eighteen, he wrote the famous song 'Only Our Rivers Run Free'. For many years he was a newspaperman in Dublin, but he now lives with his wife and daughters in Listowel, Co. Kerry, where he concentrates on his music, recording the occasional album of his songs. He keeps his journalistic hand in with a regular opinion column in The Kerryman.

THE MAN WHO DRANK THE FARM

My Uncle Peter rolled his eyes and gave out a mighty roar,
He grasped his chest, he gasped for breath and he fell dead on
  the floor.
Then later, when the will was read, the family was alarmed
For Uncle Peter left to me his house and farm of land.

Now I was never into farming much, to the soil I don't belong.
I much prefer the public house with the wimmin, wine and song.
That's why the neighbours point at me and say behind their hands,
'Sure yonder goes Mad Mickey, he's the man who drank the farm.'

And first I drank the bottom field and then I drank the bog,
Forty little black faced ewes and Shep the collie dog,
The cattle in the byre, the bonhams and the sow,
Now I've finished with the harrow and I'm starting on the plough.

Now Hector was the bantam cock and he
  was the first to go—
For long before the crack of dawn he'd
  stick up his beak and crow.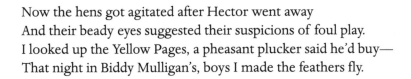
A neighbour woman up the road admired
  him in the yard,
So two pounds fifty later and bould Hector
  got his cards.

Now the hens got agitated after Hector went away
And their beady eyes suggested their suspicions of foul play.
I looked up the Yellow Pages, a pheasant plucker said he'd buy—
That night in Biddy Mulligan's, boys I made the feathers fly.

Then a few old friends invited me to a soccer match in Spain,
So a load of bullocks later and I climbed aboard the plane.

I must have took the long way home for I wakened up in Greece
Where I found that bed and breakfast cost me cutlets, chops
  and fleece.

Mind you, sheep are awful awkward yokes, for when they choose
  to graze
They insist on climbing to the tops of mountains, hills and braes.
When I heard that the All-Ireland was being held in Ballina
Without the slightest hesitation, I flogged the flock to fund
  the Fleadh.

Now the bank is getting nasty and they say they'll take no more
And have started pinning statements with sharp daggers to the door.
They say when they come round again, they'll bring the bailiffs in
So it looks as if I'm facing Ruination Once Again.

    Ruination Once Again
    Ruination Once Again
    Without another load of bullocks, it's
    Ruination Once Again.

Now things are getting desperate 'cause there's nothing left to sell,
But to my joy I hear that Uncle Pat is quite unwell.
I think I'll call to see him with strong drink to ease his pain,
And if Lady Luck smiles down on me, I'm in business once again.

So first I'll drink his bottom field and then I'll drink his bog,
His forty little black faced ewes and his little hairy dog,
The cattle in his byre, his bonhams and his sow—
For I will and I must get plastered for the humour is on me now!

W.F. Marshall

Born in Omagh, W.F. Marshall (1888–1959) was a Presbyterian Minister in Sixmilecross in Co. Tyrone, moving in 1928 to Castlerock, Co. Londonderry. By then his popular verses had gained him the informal title of 'The Bard of Tyrone'. His interest in local words and phrases also prompted him to write an Ulster version of Shakespeare's A Midsummer Night's Dream, *but that has not found favour with posterity. Nor, alas, has the dictionary he compiled of the Ulster Dialect – but then the manuscript was shredded by a puppy before it could be published, or so the story goes.*

ME AN' ME DA

I'm livin' in Drumlister,
    An' I'm gettin very oul',
I have to wear an Indian bag   *corn-sack*
    To save me from the coul'.
The deil a man in this townlan'   *not a man*
    Wos claner raired nor me,   *reared*
But I'm livin' in Drumlister
    In clabber to the knee.   *mud*

Me da lived up in Carmin,
    An' kep' a sarvint boy;
His second wife wos very sharp,
    He birried her with joy: *buried*
Now she wos thin, her name was Flynn,
    She come from Cullentra,
An' if me shirt's a clatty shirt   *dirty*
    The man to blame's me da.

Consarnin' weemin, sure it wos
    A constant word of his,

'Keep far away from them that's thin,
      Their temper's aisy riz.'
Well, I knowed two I thought wud do,
      But still I had me fears,
So I kiffled back an' forrit   *wavered*
      Between the two, for years.

Wee Margit had no fortune
      But two rosy cheeks wud plaze;
The farm of lan' wos Bridget's,
      But she tuk the pock disayse: *smallpox*
An' Margit she wos very wee,
      An' Bridget she wos stout,
But her face wos like a gaol dure
      With the bowlts pulled out.

I'll tell no lie on Margit,
      She thought the worl' of me;
I'll tell the thruth, me heart wud lep
      The sight of her to see.
But I wos slow, ye surely know,
      The raison of it now,
If I left her home from Carmin
      Me da wud rise a row.

So I swithered back an' forrit   *dithered*
      Till Margit got a man;
A fella come from Mullaslin
      An' left me jist the wan.
I mind the day she went away,
      I hid wan strucken hour,
An' cursed the wasp from Cullentra
      That made me da so sour.

But cryin' cures no trouble,
  To Bridget I went back,
An' faced her for it that night week
  Beside her own thurf-stack.
I axed her there, an' spoke her fair,
  The handy wife she'd make me,
I talked about the lan' that joined
  – Begob, she wudn't take me!

    So I'm livin' in Drumlister,
      An' I'm getting' very oul'
    I creep to Carmin wanst a month
      To thry an' make me sowl:
    The deil a man in this townlan'
      Wos claner raired nor me,
    An' I'm livin' in Drumlister
      In clabber to the knee.

Seán Masterson

Seán Masterson is from Cornafean, Co. Cavan. He has written many an ode in celebration of his native patch, including one about the village's new Millennium Monument. This, however, is a far more grisly tale. It appears in volume two of Songs of the Winding Erne *(1994), Seán McElgunn's lively anthology of ballads and other verses from the Cavan–Fermanagh border country. One can only hope that the poem's title (which means 'A Grain of Salt') is meant to be taken in more ways than one.*

GRANUM SALIS

My schooldays were full of confusion
I wasn't bright, I'm tellin the truth
My parents came to the conclusion
That I wasn't fit for Maynooth.
Too tall for a dwarf in a circus
And much too short for the Guards
An in-between ignorant gosson   *boy*
Ill-designed for financial rewards.
But my Father thought I was a charmer
And in this verse I'm going to explain—
He sent me to work for a farmer
In a backward place called Cornafean.

Now this man had no sister or brother
And he must have been sixty or more
And he lived with his old widowed mother
An invalid of ninety-four.

79

The first week it wasn't too easy
I couldn't do anything right
And the grub it was never too greasy
It was stirabout morning and night.

The dinner had few variations
Not a word about mutton or malt
One day it was salt and potatoes
The next day, potatoes and salt.
Then there was a slight improvement
Three chickens, they died in the coop
We et the mate out of the feathers
And lived for a week on the soup.
Then it was all vegetation
Turnips and cabbage, aye and grass
Not very high-calorie rations
Till misfortune befell the oul ass.

One morning I went to catch Walter
That was the oul donkey's name
And the minute I put on the winkers
I could see he was terrible lame.
I ran back and I told the farmer
And he vitted him crooked and straight   *examined*
And he whispered to me with a murmur
Ah there's no use in wastin good mate.
He sent me home for the mallet
The big butcher's knife and the saw
And the ass he gave a huge tremor
When he stuck the big knife in his craw.

He then wiped the knife in his britches
Saying that's the last journey for Walt
He split the ass down the middle

And he sent me to town for the salt.
Now the mate of an ass is like rubber
Not fit for a stomach like mine
But the farmer had teeth like a grubber   *harrow*
And he et him clane out of the brine.

I gave a piece to the granny
I thought it might help her improve
But that night she lay roarin for Andrews   *(Liver Salts)*
It was to keep the oul ass on the move.
The farmer he slept in the kitchen
In a big settle-bed with two doors
For his pillow the straddle and britchin   *saddle / breech-band*
and he'd waken the dead with his snores.

The old woman was a slave to sciatic
She couldn't lie aisy in bed
When at night I'd retire to the attic
She'd be sittin there noddin her head.
One morning I woke in the gable
And I came down the stairs in surprise
Wasn't the old woman laid out on the table
And your man was there closin her eyes.

I ran out the door like a demon
And he was shoutin to halt
As I flew down the road he was roarin
'Will yah come back here and get me the salt.'

W. Mellor

Another trouvaille *from the Meharg collection. All over Ireland, local verses of this sort are still being written, drawing on (and preserving) the comic details and small dramas that are the real stuff of rural life. Though often lacking the polish and grammatical rectitude that publishers and critics usually demand of poetry, this creative tradition of verse is quite another breed of animal, in its own way an entirely admirable one, and it would be wrong to dismiss it.*

All we know about the writer is that he came from Ballyeaston in Co. Antrim, and that he died in 1982. Here, with sympathy and charm, he allows us a glimpse into lives that are both as odd and as ordinary as any we will ever encounter, all told with an artlessness that takes from technique the minimum required for the task.

THE BALLYBOLEY BUDGIE SHOW, 1953

In Lower Ballyboley there met one summer's day
Fanciers of the feathered race, their budgies
    to display;
The birds were brought by motor car from
    Doagh and Ballyclare
And many others too many for me to declare.

The judge was Mr Bellingham, a man of
    renown,
While a watchful eye was kept on him by men
    from Belfast town.
Moore and Snoddy were there: they were two
    you'll agree
Know a budgie with anyone no matter who
    they be.

Judging started at five o'clock, no finer sight I've seen
Than those birds in their splendour, yellow, blue and green;
When the judging it was o'er, we had a cup of tea,
Nicely brewed and handed round by members of the
    ladies' committee.

Without ladies you'll agree, man surely would be lost
For the ladies are the life of men, no matter what the cost;
After tea we had refreshments, brandy, lemonade and beer—
But Snoddy said the beer was bad, it made him feel so queer.

It made him see two budgies where there was only one,
And Davie Moore could only laugh: beer makes him full of fun.
Now, the fanciers, I am sad to say, have lost a faithful member,
For Johnny Gilmour has sold his birds and bought a gander.

A gander and a turkey hen, these two he'll cross I know
And in the future he will have some grey wings for our show,
But I must finish this little rhyme and thank you one and all,
For the hospitality I was shown in Ballyboley's Old School Hall.

Anonymous

'My Aunt Jane' is a children's street song. It is the sole representative in these pages of a branch of verse-making, still lively in Ulster, that includes skipping-rhymes, playground counting-games, comic anecdotes and jokes in rhyme, and of course mocking chants to tease or torment friends and enemies alike. This particular example revolves around an enthusiasm universally shared by the young – sweets. The goodies named would probably allow a historian of confectionery to pinpoint when these atmospheric lines first came into being.

MY AUNT JANE

My aunt Jane, she took me in
She gave me tea out o' her wee tin
Half a bap and a wee snow top
And cinnamon buds out o' her wee shop.

My aunt Jane has a bell at the door
A white step-stone and a clean-swept floor
Candy-apples and hard green pears
And conversation lozengers.

My aunt Jane can dance a jig,
And sing a ballad round a sweetie pig
Wee red eyes, and a cord for a tail
Hanging in a bunch from a farthing nail.

My aunt Jane she's awful smart
She bakes a ring in an apple tart
And when that Hallow E'en comes around
Fornenst that tart I'm always found.   *in front of*

James O'Kane

In 1938, the London firm of A.H. Stockwell published Michael Hurl's post-humous edition of the work of James O'Kane (1832–1913), entitled Country Poems and Ballads: Versified Humour and Sentiment of the Ulster Countryside in the 'Brave Days of Old'.

Despite the book's uninspiring subtitle, O'Kane, a small farmer from Gortnure, Swatragh, in the south of Co. Derry, was far more than a comic or sentimental versifier. In the 1880s, for example, during the Irish Land War (which eventually led to the collapse of the landlord system), he advocated in his work the rights of Ulster's tenant farmers. Known as 'The Bard of Carntogher', he was always a meticulous literary craftsman, paying close attention to the mechanics of rhythm and rhyme. And even in his light-hearted poems (like the one below) about life in the townlands and small towns of the province, his beautifully phrased and balanced verses are also valuable social documents – in verse 4, for example, note the 'understrapper', an apprentice market official, who is evidently wearing his father's coat.

THE GRASS-SEED MARKET

When you have seen the Wild West Show
An' the great Fair of Ballinasloe,
To Maghera next Thursday go
    An' see the Grass-Seed Market.

Here horses, donkeys, mules an' nags
Come up from bogs an' down from crags,
With carts an' cars heaped high with bags
     Of grass-seed for the Market.

All sorts of seed are here displayed—
For every farmer's in the trade—
An' various samples are arrayed
     Before you in the Market.
        An' when the buyer does appear,
        A pencil stuck behin' his ear ,
        He carries in his hand a spear
           For probin' in the Market.

        An' as he shakes it on his cuff
        He calls your seed inferior stuff,
        An' says in accents loud an' gruff,
          'A rather hairy Market.'   *chancy*
          Indeed, in truth I'm boun' to say
          There's sorts of seed for sale to-day,
          A whiff of wind would blow away
            An' blind you in the Market.

The 'understrapper' first goes roun',
With overcoat that sweeps the groun',
His business is to 'beat you down'
     Before they start the Market;
An' old an' young, morose an' gay,
They'd like to buy but cannot pay;
They probe your bag an' move away
     Like spectres through the Market.

Now, if the grass-seed price is low
The farmer's face will tell you so—

He ups an' says, 'I think I'll go
     An' leave this Grass-Seed Market.'
But if it happens to be dear
His smile extends from ear to ear,
He seeks his friends an' stan's them beer
     An' whiskey in the Market.

One evenin' as I strolled along
I thought I heard a woman's tongue,
The words she used were loud an' strong,
     I couldn't but remark it.
She wheeled a barrow down the street,
An' in it lay a man complete,
Said she, 'My husban' lost his feet
     Outside the Grass-Seed Market.

He got excited on the War,
An' started one in Walsh's Bar,
An' swore he saw the oul' Tiz-ar
     Recruitin' in the Market.
But, morya, when we get as far
As home, bedad, I'll give him war—
The divil take the oul' Tiz-ar
     An' *damn* the Grass-Seed Market!'

Anonymous

JWJ: The instant I spotted the verses below hanging up in the smallest room of my co-editor's house, I knew that they demanded a place here too. They were written to commemorate the arrival in Glenarm of Hector's grandfather, Randal Mark Kerr McDonnell, Viscount Dunluce, born at St James's Palace in London three months before, in December 1878. Hector explained that somehow he hadn't liked to suggest them for our book. I wouldn't take no for an answer.

In these egalitarian times it is hard to appreciate that landlords in Ireland might ever have enjoyed a harmonious, even loving, relationship with their tenantry. Hector's forebears certainly did so, in accordance with a social order that seemed to be sanctioned by God Himself. Nonetheless, the unknown poet (who signed himself simply 'H.M.') was not shy to hint that, as the carriage bearing the Antrims rolled by, a simple wave of the hand would have been greatly appreciated by those who had turned out to welcome the baby home. But perhaps the future 7th Earl of Antrim needed to have his nappy changed, and they couldn't wait to get to the family seat – a seat which, as a local newspaper would later report, was 'teeming with history'.

ON THE ARRIVAL OF THE EARL AND COUNTESS OF ANTRIM WITH THEIR FIRST BORN SON IN GLENARM

The Antrim Heir arrived to-day,
　　With neither pomp nor show,
Tho' there was no outward WELCOME,
　　Yet our hearts were all aglow.

No arches spanned our Village Streets,
　　With scrolls of WELCOME on;
No shouts of greeting met the heir
　　As the carriage rolled along.

Still everyone did seem rejoiced
　　As the carriage drew more near,
Which bore the Little Stranger home
　　To us all so very dear.

'Twas not for lack of loyalty
　　To Antrim's Ancient Line,
We wanted but the signal
　　For loyalty to shine.

We waited but the signal
　　Our love for to display,
We have every wish to honour him,
　　Son of Antrim and of Grey.

God bless the Antrims one and all
　　Long live their Little Heir,
'Tis the wish of all their tenants,
　　And still shall be their prayer.

God bless the Lady Sybil too,
　　So gentle and so fair;

We love her equally the same
    Though she was not born an heir.

May she grow like her Grandmamma,
    The Dowager Countess Jane;
For goodness and charity
    Are blended with her name.

May Earl and Countess both live long
    And their Little Son we pray,
May they follow in the footsteps
    Of the dear ones gone away.

Moira O'Neill

Moira O'Neill (1865–1955) is remembered today for her once wildly popular
Songs of the Glens of Antrim *(1901). The name is a pseudonym: she was
born Agnes Nesta Shakespeare Higginson, and grew up in Cushendun, Co.
Antrim, where as a child she picked up many dialect words – such as the
balorin' ('yelling') of verse three below. She married into the southern Irish
ascendancy family of Skrine.*

*The novelist Molly Keane, who was one of her children, later recalled
that as a child she saw little of her mother, since most of the actual mother-
ing in the family was left to a nanny. While away at boarding school in her
teens, however, 'letters from my mother brought on such spasms of emotion
as to make them almost unwelcome'. The poem here is strikingly similar in
theme to more than one of Molly Keane's novels of family life in the 'Big
House' – though the social context could hardly be more different.*

NEVER MARRIED

My mother had three daughters, an' the ouldest one was me,
    The other two was married in their youth;
'Tis well for them that likes it, but by all that I could see
    It 'ud never fit meself, an' there's the truth.

Oh, never think I'm wantin' to miscall the race o' men,
    There's not a taste o' harm in them, the cratures!
They're meddlesome, an' quarrelsome, an' troublesome, but then
    The Man Above He put it in their natures.

I'd never be uncivil, sure an' marriage must be right,
    Or what 'ud bring the childer to the fore?
Wid their screechin' an' their roarin' an' balorin' day an' night,—
    Me sister Ann has five, an' Jane has more.

I couldn't work wid childer, an' the men's a bigger kind,
 But muddy an' mis*chee*vous like the small;
Ye've got to larn them betther, an' ye've got to make them mind,
 An' ye've got to keep them aisy afther all.

I'm betther doin' wi' dumb things, a weeny black-face lamb,
 Or the yaller goosey-goslins on the knowe;   *hilltop*
The neighbours think I'm sensible wi' sick ones, so I am,—
 Sure 'twas me that saved the life o' Mullen's cow.

Aye, ye'll often hear them say a woman cannot bide her lone,
 An' it's fifty years alone that I have bided;
They're very apt to say no woman yet could guide her own,—
 But them that God guides is well guided!

Hugh Porter

Known as 'The Bard of Moneyslane' after his home in Co. Down, Hugh Porter (1780–1839) was one of the best of the 'Rhyming Weavers'. Despite a humble background, he attracted the attentions of the local rector, who spread the word about the gifted poet that he had discovered. Eventually, in 1813, a volume of Porter's work was issued, which the poet entitled Poetical Attempts. *The modesty of the book's title was symptomatic of the man – as can be seen in the final verse of the following highly accomplished poem, which reveals Porter's views on almost everything he judged to be important.*

THE MAKING OF A MAN

The King on a throne, who can set
    himself down,
Belov'd by the people of country and town,
May say for a certainty, sure of renown,
    It's monarchy makes the man.

The Statesman will study to settle such laws,
As may from the house gain the loudest applause,
For then they will tell him in hearty huzzas,
    It's policy makes the man.

The Gallant and Gentleman often combine,
In praise of the comforts of women and wine;
They'll say at assemblies and balls, where they shine,
    It's pleasure that makes the man.

The Minister piously preaches and prays,
And bids us be mindful to mend in our ways;
Then nods with his head, and most solemnly says,
    Religion still makes the man.

The Scholar, who fondly would feast on the foliage,
That springs from the ever-green branches of
    knowledge,
Cries as he comes home in a fuss from the college,
    It's learning that makes the man.

The Poet sits puzzling all night o'er his pen,
Here scribbling a sentence, there blotting out ten;
And if he succeed, as he seldom does, then
    It's nature that makes the man.

The Quack, if he visit you, talks about nought,
So much as the wonderful cures he has wrought,
He'll bid you of laud'num take daily a draught,
    For medicine makes the man.

The Soldier surrounded by foes in a ring,
Can die like a hero, triumphant, and sing,
O death! what art thou to my country and King?
    It's honour that makes the man.

The Beau struts about every day in his best;
His soul is well pleased, when his body's well dress'd;
He says, when he looks at his fine silken vest,
    It's clothing that makes the man.

The Gamester, who often addresses the ninny,
With – sir, you have spirit, you'll play for a guinea;
Will shout, when he tricks him out of his last penny,
    It's fortune that makes the man.

The Drunkard who all he can scramble up drinks,
And cares not a farthing what swims or what sinks;
In spite of religion and reason, still thinks,
    It's whiskey that makes the man.

The Glutton has ever an appetite, able
To equal the best epicure at the table;
He'll tell you that abstinence is but a fable,
    It's mutton that makes the man.

The Miser, full fifty feet deep in a delf,   *pit*
Will plunge for a penny to put to his pelf;   *wealth*
Then joyfully count it, and say to himself,
    It's money that makes the man.

Another poor wretch, but I know not his name,
Lives hid in obscurity, shut out from fame,
And thinks that assurance is only a shame;
    When modesty makes the man.

The Beggar cries as he comes up to the door,
O, Sir, would you lend a relief to the poor?
It's only but lent, for we're all
  very sure
    It's charity makes the man.

The Pick-pocket cries, he is rob'd in the fair,
The Cozener – he's cheated will solemnly swear;
And a Thief will be ever the first to declare
    It's honesty makes the man.

But now in conclusion, observe by the way,
If these verses live but a year and a day,
Along with their Author, I'm certain you'll say,
    It's nonsense that makes the man.

For some reason, probably a surfeit of funerals, members of the clergy are often devotees of the minor genre of the unflattering memorial verse. It may have been Porter's friendship with the rector of Moneyshane that gave him the habit of composing them. Here are some examples, taken from Ian Adamson's excellent selection, The Country Rhymes of Hugh Porter *(1992).*

FOUR EPITAPHS

EPITAPH ON A MISER

He's flitted, an' whether for waur or for better,
We canna weel say, nor it's no muckle matter;   *it's no big thing*
But this we can safely assert, without study,
A narrower saul never fled frae a body.

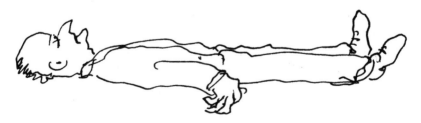

ANOTHER

His Body's buried here,
    And how his spirit fares,
I canna say – but this I'll swear:
    There's nane that kent him, cares.   *knew*

ON A SPENDTHRIFT

Below this bit slate
    He lies lifeless and caul,
That drank an estate,
    An' was dry after all.

ON A SLUGGARD

He's dead, an' he's rotten, and few for him weepin';
    He couldna be bother'd wi' breath:
He was so extremely delighted wi' sleepin',
    He's lien down to doze here wi' death.

Billy Ritchie

*Through all the years of pain and trouble suffered over the last century in
Ulster, it was easy to forget that almost everyone was kind, decent and gener-
ous at heart, irrespective of political or religious allegiances. But the motives
of strangers are easily misunderstood, and prejudices may be confirmed by*

simple breakdowns in communication. 'Paddy's Prayer' neatly illustrates the sort of thing that can go wrong. The verses were published in 1996, in Doreen McBride's book of recitations, Great Verse to Stand up and Tell Them.

PADDY'S PRAYER

Paddy was a Catholic and a man of simple ways
With a Faith that seemed to carry him through life,
Emphatically believing that he who stops and prays,
Would get his needs in times of pressing strife.

When at one time Pat's affairs got something out of hand.
You may find his course of action rather odd,
But he wanted to put through a plea with no hint of demand
And so he wrote a letter straight to God.

'Dear Father, up in Heaven, You will know my need is dire,
So I trust on my request You will not frown,
But I work out at the moment that the least I do require
And appeal to You to grant is fifty pound.'

Then he popped it in the postbox thinking, 'He will find a way.'
On the envelope he simply wrote 'To God.'
In the due course it was lifted by the middle of next day
By the postman, Billy Mac, who was a Prod!

Now Billy bein' a member of the local Orange Lodge
Brought the matter to a meeting for to press.
'If our hearts are set in charity, let's not the issue dodge,
Can't we help Paddy in his dark distress?

For although he is a Catholic, he's still a decent lad,
I'm sure you all know him as well as I.
If we can't make an effort, then I'd say it's rather sad
And though funds are low, it's only right to try!'

Well the matter was debated and got nearly shelved away
While charity with funding had to strive,
Until it was decided by all present there that day
That the best that they could do was 'twenty-five'.

So the cash was sent to Paddy with a note to wish him well,
On the headed paper of the orange and blue,
Expressing their desiring of his worries for to quell
And hoping that perhaps 'twould see him through.

As Pat strolled on the roadway in a further seven days,
He met Seamus, whom he'd told about his plan.
'Just how has it been going?' with a twinkle Seamus says,
'How'd you get on with your letter till Yer Man?

Did you get help like you asked for in answer to your prayer?'
Says Pat, 'I knew He'd help me if He could
For He always has responded to a justified affair
And He sent help to me like I knew He would.

Still His wisdom I now question and my faith begins to fall
And with me you'll know for certain that's no laugh,
For He sent it through the brethren of the local Orange Hall,
And would you believe? The buggers kept the half!'

Anonymous

This gruesome set of verses is something out of the ordinary. Never before in print, as far as we can establish, it was found on a sheet of paper among the late Mat Meharg's cache of favourite pieces.

ROBERT RITCHIE, SWINE BUTCHER

Hark! I hear an awful yelling
At the rear of yonder dwelling!
I guess it's Robert Ritchie felling
Pigs.

See his onward step advance:
Within the sheath he bears the lance
Which puts the jurries in a trance: *pigs*
Bob Ritchie.

He takes the sledge within his hands
Close by the pig he ready stands,
Soon it falls by those commands:
Bob Ritchie.

Then the knife he uses quick,
And in its throat he does it stick,
He holds the legs lest they should kick:
Bob Ritchie.

Now when the blood has ceased to flow
He lets the limbs of jurry go,
Then, at the shaving, to and fro,
It is Bob Ritchie.

He's quite an expert at the job,
He never heeds poor jurry's sob,
More boiling water bring to Bob,
Yes, Ritchie.

And when the shaving's done quite neat
He ties it up by its hind feet,
And very soon the job's complete,
By Ritchie.

The knife is thrust into the gut
And all the organs pulled or cut,
The job is finished now all but
The toilet needs of Ritchie.

He washes up the sharp edged tools,
And pays attention to his rules:
You'll find he's none of God's damned fools,
Bob Ritchie.

So last of all we see him splatter
And plunge his hands within the water.
He'll spin a yarn, it does not matter—
Where is Bob Ritchie?

Amanda M'Kittrick Ros

That irascible schoolmistress from the Antrim town of Larne, Mrs Amanda M'Kittrick Ros (1860–1939), wrote several novels, and it is on those exuberant displays of literary camp that her reputation (or notoriety) rides. Her collections of verse, Poems of Puncture *(1913) and* Fumes of Formation *(1933), are more muted, but they too have their moments of blossoming bliss.*

THE OLD HOME

Don't I see the old home over there at the base
Of a triangle not overcrowded with space:
'Twas there I first breathed on the eighth of December,
In the year of Our Lord the month after November.

I've been told it was snowy and blowy and wild
When I entered the home as a newly-born child,
There wasn't much fuss, nor was there much joy
For sorrow was poignant I wasn't a boy.

I felt quite contented as years flitted on
That I to the coarser sex did not belong
Little dreaming that ever the time would arrive
That of female attire I would be deprived.

By a freak of the lustful that spreads like disease
Which demanded that females wear pants if you please,
But I stuck to the decentest style of attire
And to alter my 'gender' I'll never aspire.

During that hallowed century now dead and gone
In which good Queen Victoria claimed to be born
From childhood her modesty ever was seen
Her exalted position demanded when Queen.

She set an example of decency rare,
That no English Queen before her you'd compare
Neither nude knee nor ankle, nude bosom nor arm
Dare be seen in her presence this Queen to alarm.

She believed in her sex being loving and kind,
And modesty never to march out of line
By exposing those members unrest to achieve,
Which pointed to morals immorally grave.

But sad to relate when she bade 'Adieu'
To earth and its vanities tainted with 'rue',
That centre of fashion, so French in its style,
Did its utmost to vilify decency's smile

And mock at these garments which proved in their day,
At a glance – who was who – and wherein gender lay,
But alas! Since the death of our great and good Queen
That attribute 'Modesty''s ne'er to be seen.

It wasn't long after till modesty grew
A thing of the past for me and for you;
Last century's fashions were blown quite aside,
The ill-advised folk of this age now deride.

The petticoat faded away as we do
In circumference it covered not one leg but two,
Its successor exposes the arms, breasts and necks,
Legs, knees and thighs and too often – the ——.

Amanda's husband, Andy Ross (who preferred to use both his 's's), was for some years stationmaster in Larne. A popular and convivial figure, he died in 1917, and on the day of his funeral, the sorrowing widow hired a man with a handcart to return all the wreaths that came from people she disliked. That afternoon she sat down to write a poem worthy of a great railwayman, her own tribute to the late Mr Ros – as he would now forever be.

THE ENGINEER DIVINE

Across the deep chasm which nothing can fill
Since man was from Paradise driven;
The Great Engineer with remarkable skill,
Constructed a railway to Heaven.

The Span of the Bridge is a wonder
   of strength
And of sightless beauty combined.
Its dimensions in breadth and ditto in length,
The Master of All hath designed.

The wires of communion, extended with care,
From Earth to the Station above:
The current of faith from the battery of prayer,
Can act on the Magnet of Love.
With movements produced by a Motor Divine
Which matchless perfection displays,
The Engine of Truth as it runs up the line
The Train of Salvation conveys.

It wasn't often that Amanda could bear to write in praise of her native land. Here she does so, though perhaps the effort was too great to sustain. After the resounding beginning, the last line is a masterpiece of bathos.

OLD IRELAND

O Island of Verdure! and Saints who were dear,
Now gone to reside in a far better sphere,
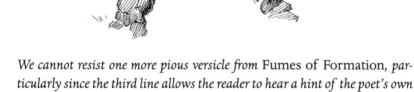
So loved by our ancestors ere we were born
We would die to protect you from insult and
    scorn.
Sweet Ireland I love with its fields ever green
Umbrelled with blue by a Maker Unseen:
One time you were studded with castles
    throughout,
But now of this fact – a stranger would doubt.

We cannot resist one more pious versicle from Fumes of Formation, *particularly since the third line allows the reader to hear a hint of the poet's own carefully cultivated voice.*

LOVE

Love is pleasing – moreso money
    Powerful factor – life's best honey;
Super far the gift of God
    To a world of sin and fraud.

Richard Rowley

Under his real name, Richard Valentine Williams (1877–1947) was a minor industrialist until his fifties, when the family firm of cotton manufacturers had to close. But as the poet Richard Rowley he was known and loved by many. In the 1940s, he set up a small press and began to offer a friendly ear – and sometimes even publication – to the neglected writers of Ulster, who would never forget him.

Rowley's own early poems were of Belfast – such as 'The Islandmen', which spoke of the noble army of workers tramping over the bridge each day to the great city shipyard. He set most of his later verses, like the one here, in the Ulster countryside, issuing them himself in collections such as Ballads of Mourne *(1940).*

POACHIN' TOM

The Earl he has his mountains,
His deer-park an' demesne,
His grouse upon the heather,
His partridge in the grain,
His trout in lake or river,
An' salmon from the sea.
Och, sport must cost him gold galore,
But all mine's free.

In Slieve-na-Slat at midnight
I wire a cunnin' snare,
Sure that I'll find at dawnin'
A rabbit or a hare.
In Altnadua Lake at dusk
I drop my baited line,
An' ere the dark is lifted
The best o' trout is mine.

Thro' the forests of winter
Down by Burren Bog,
I hide myself behind the reeds
Wi' my gun and dog.
Ice twinkles on the water,
The moon shines in the sky,
Then wi' a rush an' whirr o' wings,
The ducks comes by.

God made the mountains,
An' God made the game;
If I take my share o' them,
Am I much to blame?
Some fancies money,
Some courts a girl;
I'm all for sport myself,
Just like the Earl!

James H. Scott
(Attrib.)

In the spring of 1940 these irresistible lines appeared in the New Northman, *over the initials 'J.H.S.' Assuming that they were not written by the only other poet we can think of who composed 'hums', Winnie-the-Pooh – who was never at Queen's University, Belfast – it seems very probable that they were the work of the much-loved James Henderson Scott (1913–70) of the Anatomy Department there. Dr Scott was a brilliant, if idiosyncratic teacher – he used to lecture in total darkness to stop his students taking notes. He was also a keen poet all his life: when in 1964 he became Professor of Dental Anatomy at Queen's, he even delivered his inaugural address in iambic hexameters.*

NONSENSE HUM

Take ten thousand pudding pots
And place them upside down,
On each grow grass and plant tall trees
That sing in every passing breeze,

And here and there a little town,
With small white houses, tiny streams,
And over all the old sad dreams ...
So God made County Down.

Elizabeth Shane

'Elizabeth Shane' is a pseudonym – her real name was Gertrude Hind (1877–1951). A poet and playwright, she was also a keen amateur yachtswoman, sailing out of Carrickfergus. As a musician, she became first violinist with the Belfast Philharmonic. Later in life, she transferred her poetical affections west from her native Co. Down to the Donegal coast (which she honoured in the titles of two of her three books of verse).

Above all, it is her poem 'Wee Hughie' that has lasted. In the 1940s, it was set to music by John Larchet, and it became part of the repertoire of the popular Hogmanay tenor Kenneth McKellar. The verses may be accused of sentimentality, but – certainly if you have your own children – the emotions they describe are real enough.

WEE HUGHIE

He's gone to school, Wee Hughie,
An' him not four,
Sure I saw the fright was in him,
When he left the door.

But he took a hand o' Denny
An' a hand o' Dan,
Wi' Joe's owld coat upon him—
Och, the poor wee man!

He cut the quarest figure,
More stout nor thin;
An' trottin' right an' steady
Wi' his toes turned in.

I watched him to the corner
O' the big turf stack,
An' the more his feet went forrit,
Still his head turned back.

He was lookin', would I call him—
Och, my heart was woe—
Sure it's lost I am without him,
But he be to go.

I followed to the turnin'
When they passed it by,
God help him, he was cryin',
An', maybe, so was I.

James Simmons

A characteristically dry observation by the poet James Simmons (1933–2001), taken from his collection, Poems 1956–1986. *Never an advocate of self-consciously literary writing, all his creative life Simmons was a powerful force for the good in Ulster poetry and prose, founding the province's first essential 'little magazine',* The Honest Ulsterman, *and even recording refreshingly unpretentious albums of his own songs.*

EPIGRAM

When I had curls
I knew more girls.
I do more reading
now my hair is receding.

William R. Stewart

As shrewd readers may guess, these verses come from Mat Meharg's collection. Not very much is known about the background to this tribute to the Meharg family business, but their composer, Willie Stewart, lived in Carnlough, Co. Antrim, some ten miles away from Ballyboley, which was their centre of operations. Willie was well known in the neighbourhood as a collector of fossils and a producer of humorous verses. He would turn out the latter on request to enliven local occasions, but in spite of this his eulogy to the Mehargs seems to be the only one of his poems that has survived.

THE MEHARG BROTHERS

When your car needs some repairs,
You'll want your job well done:

Try Meharg's, that well known firm,
Where famous men do come.
There're four of them, all bright and gay,
Light-hearted and so kind;
Their courtesy is wonderful,
No better you could find.

Where are you going? Give me your hand;
Come along with me—
You will never regret the day
The Mehargs you went to see.

There's Bobbie, and there's brother John,
There's Davey and there's Mat,
To search the place for miles around,
You'd find no better lot:
Their taxis are at your command,
As soon as you arrange a date,
You'll hear the boys declare—
Jump in or we'll be late!

Where are you going? Give me your hand;
Come along with me—

You will never regret the day
The Mehargs you went to see.

If ever you go for a drive,
You'll find their company grand;
They're sure to point out ancient things,
As they drive o'er the land;
Their knowledge is so wonderful,
Of places far and near,
So just sit back and quiet be,
And this is what you'll hear:

Where are you going? Give me your hand;
Come along with me—
You will never regret the day
The Mehargs you went to see.

Anonymous

If fourteen lines make a sonnet, then the poem below must be one. Like William Stewart's verses above, this uncredited discovery comes from the Meharg box, though it concerns a different aspect of Antrim working life, the art of road-surfacing. The Kelly with a walk-on part in the second verse is certainly Jimmy Kelly, the reciting roadmender of Glenarm – who appears as a poet in his own right in Ireland's Other Poetry: Anonymous to Zozimus.

THE TAR ENGINE ON THE COAST ROAD

Close by where runs the brimming tide by sweet Glenarm Bay
The tarring work is going on without the least delay.

The engine she is running clear at fifteen knots or more—
I wish that you could only hear the radiator roar.
The bonnet rattles to and fro, the skip is running free:
I say for fun that she might run for all eternity.

The men are working hard below, the sweat runs down their face,
They call aloud to Kelly to slacken down the pace;
But I must keep going on when the weather it is dry
And mix the stuff together that is the real McKay.
If by chance my engine breaks I'll ring you on the phone—
A pretty spot it is to be stranded here alone.

Goodbye then for the present, I hope we'll meet soon again,
And always have a foreman as good as Mr Maine.

W.M. Thackeray

The writer and artist William Makepeace Thackeray (1811–63) was English, and where Ireland was concerned he had a singularly inappropriate middle name. After his Irish Sketch Book *came out in 1843 – with the verses below in it – he protested that everyone attacked him for being anti-Irish when he had simply told the truth. An Irish coachman once waved the book at him, growling, 'You hate us, Mr Thackeray.' The author just sighed, 'God help me, when all I ever loved was Irish!'*

Certainly, Mrs Thackeray was, though she did not seem to be very fond of her native land. Indeed, her husband's first attempt to write the book was aborted before it began when she jumped into the sea from the Cork ferry on the way there.

In 'Peg of Limavaddy', Thackeray has returned to Ireland on his own. He is lonely – and particularly susceptible to feminine charms. Though he invokes both Homer and the famous barrister Sergeant Taddy, his real inspiration is a song called 'Kitty of Coleraine', about a pretty girl who attracts a suitor when she spills a jug of buttermilk. The poet attempts a similar ploy here. Sadly, his 'accident' attracts only laughter from Peg, and the artfully directed dowsing does nothing to cool his hopeful ardour as he sketches her.

from PEG OF LIMAVADDY

Riding from Coleraine
    (Famed for lovely Kitty),
Came a Cockney bound
    Unto Derry city,
Weary was his soul,
    Shivering and sad he
Bumped along the road
    Leads to Limavaddy.

Limavaddy inn's
    But a humble baithouse,   *eaterie*
Where you may procure
    Whiskey and potatoes;
Landlord at the door
    Gives a smiling welcome
To the shivering wights
    Who to his hotel come.
Landlady within
    Sits and knits a stocking,
With a wary foot
    Baby's cradle rocking.

Presently a maid
    Enters with the liquor
(Half a pint of ale
    Frothing in a beaker).
Gods! I didn't know
    What my beating heart meant,
Hebe's self I thought
    Enter'd the apartment.
As she came she smiled,
    And the smile bewitching,
On my word and honour,
    Lighted all the kitchen!

With a curtsey neat
    Greeting the new comer,
Lovely, smiling Peg
    Offers me the rummer;   *tumbler*
But my trembling hand
    Up the beaker tilted,
And the glass of ale
    Every drop I spilt it:
Spilt it every drop
    (Dames, who read my volumes,
Pardon such a word)
    On my whatd'yecall'ems!

Witnessing the sight
            Of that dire disaster,
Out began to laugh
            Missis, maid, and master;
Such a merry peal,
            'Specially Miss Peg's was
(As the glass of ale
            Trickling down my legs was),
That the joyful sound
            Of that ringing laughter
Echoed in my ears
            Many a long day after.

When the laugh was done,
            Peg, the pretty hussy,
Moved about the room
            Wonderfully busy;
Now she looks to see
            If the kettle keep hot,
Now she rubs the spoons,
            Now she cleans the teapot;
Now she sets the cups
            Trimly and secure,
Now she scours a pot
            And so it was I drew her.

Thus it was I drew her
            Scouring of a kettle,
(Faith! her blushing cheeks
            Redden'd on the metal!)
Ah! but 'tis in vain
            That I try to sketch it;
The pot perhaps is like,
            But Peggy's face is wretched.

No: the best of lead,
    And of Indian-rubber,
Never could depict
    That sweet kettle-scrubber!

Citizen or squire,
    Tory, Whig, or Radi-
cal would all desire
    Peg of Limavaddy.
Had I Homer's fire,
    Or that of Sergeant Taddy,
Meetly I'd admire
    Peg of Limavaddy.
And till I expire,
    Or till I grow mad, I
Will sing unto my lyre
    Peg of Limavaddy!

Anonymous

When the first successful threshing machine was invented in 1786, it did not immediately drive out the old ways of winnowing grain – see John Clifford's verses on pages 28–29. However, as this disgraceful song from not so many decades later demonstrates, some farmers passionately embraced the new technology at the earliest opportunity.

THE THRASHING MACHINE

For there was an old farmer in Down he did dwell,
He'd one pretty servant, her name it was Nell.
He'd one pretty servant she was scarce seventeen,
And he showed her the works of his thrashing machine.

Says Nell to the farmer, 'It's a fine summer's day,
While the rest of the farmers are off making hay,
Come into the barn where we won't be seen,
And the two of us start working our thrashing machine.'

Oh, Nell she stepped forward and into the house.
His boss got the harness and strapped her right on.
Nell took the handle and turned on the steam,
And the two of them started working their thrashing machine.

Oh, six months being over and nine coming on,
Nell's skirt wouldn't meet nor her drawers wouldn't go on;
It's under her oxter like a young fairy queen.
'I will have you transported for your thrashing machine.'

Oh, up comes the Judge with a pen in his claw,
He says, 'Lovely Nell, you have broken the law.'
'No, sir,' says she, 'it's plain to be seen,
I needed the strength of his thrashing machine.'

Anonymous

Seán McElgunn's 1994 anthology, Songs of the Winding Erne, *is spiced with several fragments of verse that the editor calls 'Remnants'. These enigmatic scraps have an inconsequential appeal all of their own. Here is a small selection of them:*

THREE 'REMNANTS'

Last night and the night before
Three young monkeys came to the door,
One with a flute and one with a drum
And one with a pancake stuck to his bum.

★ ★ ★

Hay and Oats
For the town goats,
Eggs and Rashers
For the country slashers.

★ ★ ★

Mary Anne Magee,
Half-past three,
She locked her door
And she turned her key.

F.F. Vint

We have not succeeded in discovering anything at all about the composer of this wry tale, though the exotic-sounding surname is not an uncommon one in Ulster. The verses were published in a half-crown pamphlet in Bangor, Co. Down, some time during the middle of the twentieth century. Called Common Sense Verse, *it seems to have been the author's only collection.*

THE WIFE

He leant upon the farmyard gate,
    And dreamt of cattle, corn and hay;
Then he espied his neighbour, John,
    Along the road making his way.

'Hi, John,' he said, 'Why in such haste?'
    Said John, 'My wife is far from well,
And I am hurrying to get
    The services of Doctor Fell.

She was took bad last afternoon,
     And from her bed she cannot stir;
I fear she's worse this morning, for
     I do not like the look of her.'

'Hold hard, until I get my hat,
     I'm with you in a moment's time;
For truly now I tell you, John,
     I simply hate the sight of mine.'

Anonymous

This thrilling account of Wun Hung Lo *and* Yankee Pete *appeared in* Pro
Tanto Quid *in 1938. It was unsigned. We can be sure that its author had read
the popular master of narrative verses, Robert Service, for in 'The Shooting of
Dan McGrew' another 'lady that's known as Lou' also causes a fight. Perhaps
the very similar anonymous classic of obscenity, 'Eskimo Nell', played a part
as well: its gunslinging 'Mexico Pete' seems to return here as a Yankee.*

THE WAY OF ALL FLESH
OR THREE MEN IN A PUB – NOT TO MENTION THE GIRL

It happened in Hong Kong one night in the House of Half Moon Joe,
The finest fight that e'er was fought in the days of long ago.
They tell the story even yet when the sailors come to drink
In the blood-stained bar where the maidens are and the guttering
     candles blink.

The toughest crews from all the world came there to drink o' nights,
And many a dirty deed was done when someone doused the lights,

And many were the maidens there, and many the things they knew,
But of all the fair there was not one there was half as sweet as Lou.

The night the dreadful deed was done was a dark and dirty night,
The rain beat down and a thunderstorm gave dashes of brilliant
    light,
And in Half Moon's House the air was thick with oaths and
    tobacco smoke—
When into the room, like the crack of doom, came a Helluva
    tough-looking bloke.

Singing a bawdy song came he as he opened wide the door,
And he said things that I cannot print as he strode across the floor.
Karl Jensen, mate of the 'Crimson Skull', a raw boned Swede was he,
With yellow hair and a glassy stare and teeth that numbered three.

He sank two brandies mighty quick and he slugged two
    whiskies slow,
Then he droitled over to where Lou sat on the knee   *staggered*
    of Wun Hung Lo;
He jerked the maiden to her feet and he kissed her on the lips.
'Let go! Let go!' cried Wun Hung Lo, and the two men came to grips.

Then over beetled Yankee Pete and slipped his arm round Lou—
At that the other two looked up, and both together said, 'You!
You blinking blanking so-and-so! You fish-faced Hound of Hell!'
And Yankee Pete rocked back on his feet, for he did not like it well.

Then Wun Hung Lo he dropped his hand and drew from his sarong
A stabbing knife with a golden hilt and a blade that was two
    feet long,
And he took his measure on Yankee's ribs to thrust it in between,
But Pete with a grunt pushed Lou in front and she took it in
    the spleen.

And Pete's arms caught her as she fell, and just before she died
He kissed her once upon the lips, and then threw her aside.
Then bending over her lovely corpse he drew out Wun Hung's knife,
He heaved a sigh as he thought 'My eye! she'd have made a right
    wee wife!'

Then he advanced on Wun Hung Lo who was now convulsed
    with fear;
And with a dexterous flick of the knife deprived him of an ear;
Then with a quiet smile on his face he spun round on his toes,
Then he made a dash and a fearful slash and cut off Jensen's nose.

Then he buried the knife in Wun Hung Lo and turned round with
    a snarl,
And using all his mighty strength pressed his thumbs on the throat
    of Karl,
But even as Jensen breathed his last, Wun Hung, at the end of
    his tether,
As he quit this life stabbed Pete with the knife – and they all
    dropped dead together.

             ★ ★ ★

Next day there were few who partook of their stew in the House
    of Half Moon Joe,
Who knew that the meat sent up by the cook from his kitchens
    down below
Consisted of Jensen and Wun Hung Lo – the juicest parts of
    the two—
And the Kidney was Pete's, and the sixpenny sweets were bits of
    the beautiful Lou.

Anonymous

The language of Ulster ballads and songs is sometimes so deeply indebted to the Anglo-Scots ('Ullans') dialect, and the ways of transcribers are so idiosyncratic, that we have not reproduced very many of them in this book. Nonetheless, 'The Wee Pickle Tow' emphatically earns its keep here – even if we may be hazy about some of the details. When Richard Hayward put the verses into his 1925 collection, Ulster Songs and Ballads of the Town and the Country, *he offered just one explanatory note: 'The word TOW must be pronounced to rhyme with NOW.' We shall curb our twitching fingers, put away the dictionaries, and follow suit.*

THE WEE PICKLE TOW

John Grumely purchased a pun o' coorse tow,
    And started his wife to the spinnin' o' it,
But a sperk frum her pipe set the tow in a low,
    An' that was the weary beginnin' o' it;
She humphed an' she grumphed, she puffed an' she flang,
She hokit, she bokit, she swore she would hang
    Before she would set to the spinnin' o' it.

Now, John, d'ye mind how our ould Mother Eve
    Was naked all at the beginnin' o' it,
But for modesty's sake wore an apron o' leaves
    An' ne'er fashed her thumbs at the spinnin' o' it;
An' if I had nine dochters as I have but three,
I'd give them advice to the day I wad dee,
    To ne'er fash their thumbs at the spinnin' o' it.

John Grumely humphed an' he sput out his chow,
    An' he called for a halter to hang her wi'
If she would nay go spin out her wee pickle tow
    An' hamper the kitchen no longer wi' it;

Ye wrinkled ould hag, there ye sit an' ye gern,
Aye, an' burn yer rock an' rayvel yer pern,
Whiles I, an ould slooter man, slappit the kern
    An' for butter, I ne'er see a blennin' o' it.

For seven long years, John, I've wanted a sark
    An' I'm sure ye ne'er heerd me complainin' o' it,
An' all of that time I have lay at your back—
    Be me mumpin' ye sure kent the meanin' o' it;
But me bairn-time's out and me pleasure's awa'.
Yer back to me waim an' yer face to the wa',
An' for that same trick damn the threed will I draw,
    An' that puts an end to the spinnin' o' it.

Ye wrinkled ould mern o' three score an' ten,
    I wunner ye have such a notion o' it,
Whiles I an ould cadger far younger nor you
    Am sure that I ne'er have a motion o' it;
But for pleasure ye've lived, for which wheen folk have died,
Whiles I am a worker, and this I decide—
There's two beds in this house, and the place we'll divide,
    And that puts an end to the spinnin' o' it.

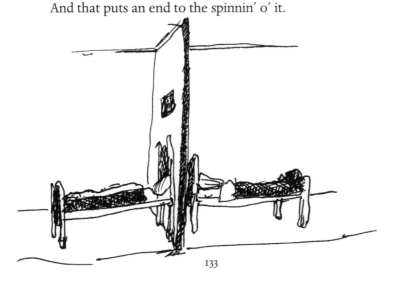

Robert Young

Robert Young (1800–c.1870), a nailer by trade from Co. Tyrone, rarely makes it into the reference books. When he does, he gets a very bad press. The Oxford Companion to Irish Literature *(1996) baldly informs us that he was 'noted for his sectarianism'. D.J. O'Donoghue is more pointed in his 1912 book,* Poets of Ireland, *where we are told that a government award of £50 a year bestowed upon him in the 1860s was 'ostensibly for literary ability, but as he had none, it must have been for political services'.*

Certainly loyalist politics pervaded Young's verses – he liked to call himself a 'Fermanagh True Blue'. But however loyal he was, without some real merit it is unlikely that he would have sold – before publication – over a thousand copies of his 1832 collection, The Orange Minstrel.

The following song of useful and practical advice for farmers makes reference in the first line to the despised Young Irelanders and their attempted rising of 1848. It was published in The Poetical Works of Robert Young of Londonderry comprising Agricultural and Miscellaneous Poems and Songs with Copious Notes *(1863). A note there informs the reader that it can be sung to the (seemingly implausible) air, 'Merrily Danced the Quaker'.*

SONG

WRITTEN ON VIEWING THE EXHIBITION OF
THE STRABANE FARMING SOCIETY IN 1848

While others are intent on war,
    The scourge of every nation,
We, at Strabane, prefer the plan
    Of rural renovation.
Improving stock, each well-bred flock
On hill and valley grazing,
Delights the eye, when passing by,
    Of all upon them gazing.

Chorus:
Then till the land with steady hand,
Forget not thorough draining,
Green crops, good grain, by it you'll gain,
Both man and beast sustaining.

Banks down may go, and merchants, though
Once rich and high in station,
From Fortune's wheel reverse may feel,
And come to ruination.
But farmers who this duty do,
And spade and plough keep going,
The stream of wealth, to cheer their health,
Will for them still be flowing.

The landlord's pride, if true and tried,
When in his carriage driving,
Should always be, in country free,
To see his tenants thriving.
A yeoman bold will law uphold,
Defying disaffection,
For Queen and State, 'gainst traitor's hate,
Be still and sure protection.

Naturally, Robert Young had detractors during his lifetime as well. He composed the lines below as a rejoinder to a claim that he could not have written an 'Elegy on the Death of Dr M'Cargill' – unless he had 'copied it out of some book, and then altered it slightly to suit his purpose'. In his 1854 collection, The Poetical Remembrancer, *the suspect elegy was immediately followed by this indignant defence.*

IMPROMPTU TO MR CHARLES AGNEW, OF STRANRAER, ON HEARING THAT HE ACCUSED THE AUTHOR OF PLAGIARISM

Sir,
I have been informed you cannot believe
That I from the Muse any favours receive;
Permit me to ask you – I mean to be brief—
From whence springs the source of your strange unbelief?

But have I said favours? – No, writing of rhyme,
For coxcombs to sneer at, although not a crime,
Is certainly folly to call it no worse,
And brings neither fame nor a coin to the purse.

Yet nature still works in the musical mind,
Although not by classical learning refin'd,
And he that without her instruction remains
Is always a dunce, though with college-gilt brains.

Now you're skill'd in lore, and to science well known,
And seem to know every man's heart but your own;
You know, sir, that learning cannot make a poet—
The gift comes from nature, none else can bestow it.

I now call upon you to mention the book
Or pages from whence I the elegy took;
Make good your assertion, it's all I require,
Else you must allow me to call you a l--r.

Mrs Cecil Frances Alexander

Having failed to locate a single poet in Ulster beginning with 'Z', we complete the alphabet by starting again at 'A'. Mrs Cecil Frances Alexander (1818–95) is best known as the writer of hymns – among them 'All Things Bright and Beautiful' and 'There is a Green Hill'. Here she turns her hand to a ballad based on a Donegal legend. It is written in a mild form of the half-Scottish speech of Ulster, versions of which we have encountered quite frequently in these pages.

These days not many readers seek out long ballads with dialect words in them. But it is worth putting aside a little time for 'The Legend of Stumpie's

Brae'. It is a grim tale, and if you read it, quite slowly, all 33 short verses of it, it will never quite leave you again. It may be that you will wish it were not so, but, deep down inside you, Stumpie will always be there, part of your very being, forever.

THE LEGEND OF STUMPIE'S BRAE

Heard ye no tell o' the Stumpie's Brae?
Sit down, sit down, young friend,
I'll make your flesh to creep to-day,
And your hair to stan' on end.

Young man, 'tis hard to strive wi' sin,
And the hardest strife of a',
Is where the greed o' gain creeps in,
And drives God's grace awa'.

Oh, it's quick to do, but it's lang to rue,
When the punishment comes at last,
And we would give the world to undo
The deed that's done and past.

Over yon strip of meadow land,
And over the burnie bright,   *stream*
Dinna ye mark the fir-trees stand,
Around yon gable white?

I mind it weel, in my younger days
The story yet was rife:
There dwelt within that lonely place
A farmer and his wife.

They sat together, all alone,
One blessed Autumn night,
When the trees without, and hedge, and stone,
Were white in the sweet moonlight.

The boys and girls were gone down all
A wee to the blacksmith's wake;   *a wee while*
There pass'd ane on by the window small,   *someone*
And guv the door a shake.

The man he up and open'd the door—
When he had spoken a bit,
A pedlar man stepp'd into the floor,
Down he tumbled the pack he bore,
Right heavy pack was it.

'Gude save us a',' says the wife, wi' a smile,
'But yours is a thrivin' trade.'—
'Ay, ay, I've wander'd mony a mile,
And plenty have I made.'

The man sat on by the dull fire flame,
When the pedlar went to rest;
Close to his ear the Devil came,
And slipp'd intil his breast.   *into*

He look'd at his wife by the dim firelight,
And she was as bad as he—
'Could we no' murder thon man the night?'—
'Ay could we, ready,' quo' she.

He took the pickaxe without a word,
Whence it stood, ahint the door;
As he pass'd in, the sleeper stirr'd,
That never waken'd more.

'He's dead!' says the auld man, coming back—
'What o' the corp, my dear?'
'We'll bury him snug in his ain bit pack,   *own little*
Never ye mind for the loss of the sack,
I've ta'en out a' the gear.'

'The pack's owre short by twa gude span,   *hand-widths*
What'll we do!' quo' he—
'Ou, you're a doited, unthoughtfu' man,   *stupid*
We'll cut him off at the knee.'

They shorten'd the corp, and they pack'd him tight,
Wi' his legs in a pickle hay;   *wee bit of*
Over the burn, in the sweet moonlight,
They carried him till this brae.   *hillside*

They shovell'd a hole right speedily,
They laid him in on his back—
'A right pair are ye,' quo' the PEDLAR, quo' he,
Sitting bolt upright in the pack.

'Ye think ye've laid me snugly here,
And none shall know my station;
But I'll hant ye far, and I'll hant ye near,
Father and son, wi' terror and fear,
To the nineteenth generation.'

The twa were sittin' the vera next night,
When the dog began to cower,
And they knew, by the pale blue firelight,
That the Evil One had power.

It had stricken nine, just nine o' the clock—
The hour when the man lay dead;
There came to the outer door a knock,
And a heavy, heavy tread.

The old man's head swam round and round,
The woman's blood 'gan freeze,
For it was not like a natural sound,
But like some one stumping o'er the ground
On the banes of his twa bare knees

And through the door, like a sough of air,
And stump, stump, round the twa,
Wi' his bloody head, and his knee banes bare—
They'd maist ha'e died of awe!   *almost*

The wife's black locks ere morn grew white,
They say, as the mountain snaws;
The man was as straight as a staff that night,
But he stoop'd when the morning rose.

Still, year and day, as the clock struck Nine,
The hour when they did the sin,
The wee bit dog began to whine,
And the ghaist came clattering in.

Ae night there was a fearful flood—
Three days the skies had pour'd;
And white wi' foam, and black wi' mud,
The burn in fury roar'd.

Quo' she – 'Gude man, ye need na turn
Sae pale in the dim firelight;
The Stumpie canna cross the burn
He'll no' be here the night.

For it's o'er the bank, and it's o'er the linn,   *stream*
And it's up to the meadow ridge'—
'Ay,' quo' the Stumpie hirpling in,   *limping*
And he gied the wife a slap on the chin,   *gave*
'But I cam' round by the bridge!'

And stump, stump, stump, to his plays again,
And o'er the stools and chairs;
Ye'd surely hae thought ten women and men
Were dancing there in pairs.

They sold their gear, and over the sea
To a foreign land they went,
Over the sea – but wha can flee
His appointed punishment?

The ship swam over the water clear,
Wi' the help o' the eastern breeze;
But the vera first sound in guilty fear,
O'er the wide, smooth deck, that fell on their ear
Was the tapping o' them twa knees.

In the woods of wild America
Their weary feet they set;

143

But Stumpie was there the first, they say,
And he haunted them onto their dying day,
And he follows their children yet.

I haud ye, never the voice of blood *tell*
Call'd from the earth in vain;
And never has crime won worldly good,
But it brought its after-pain.

This is the story o' Stumpie's Brae,
And the murderers' fearin' fate:
Young man, your face is turn'd that way,
Ye'll be ganging the night that gate. *going / that direction*

Ye'll ken it weel, through the few fir-trees,
The house where they wont to dwell;
Gin ye meet ane there, as daylight flees, *if*
Stumping about on the banes of his knees
It'll just be Stumpie himsel'.

Acknowledgments and Thanks

The Editors and Publisher offer warm thanks to the following for permission to reproduce copyright material in this book, and for their generosity. Every effort has been made to trace copyright holders, but despite strenuous researches in some cases this has proved impossible. The Publisher would be interested to hear from any copyright holders not here acknowledged.

George Barnett: 'Kelly's "Slip-Tail" Cow' from *The Wee Black Tin: Poems from Ballinascreen*, edited by Graham Mawhinney and Jennifer Johnston (Ballinascreen Historical Society 1980). / John Campbell: 'The Place' from his *Saturday Night in York Street* (Blackstaff Press, Belfast 1982); 'Faceless Magee' from his *The Rose and the Blade* (Lagan Press, Belfast 1997). / Thomas Carnduff: 'On the Night-Shift' from his *Songs of an Out-of-Work* (Quota Press, Belfast 1932). Published by permission of Sarah Ferris for the Carnduff Estate. Thomas Carnduff's papers are lodged at Queen's University, Belfast. / John Clifford: 'Wullie Boyd's Flail', by kind permission of his son, Raymond Clifford. / Albert Haslett: 'Holy Water' from his *Enjoy the Crack!* (Printneeds, Belfast ND). / Crawford Howard: 'St Patrick and the Snakes' from *Great Verse to Stand up & Tell Them* (Adare Press, Banbridge 1996); 'The Diagonal Steam Trap' from *The Crack from Belfast* (Adare Press, Banbridge 1995). / Mick McAtamney: 'The Irish Flea' from *Honey to the Ear* (Irish World Citizen Organization, South Derry Branch 1987). / Mickey MacConnell: 'The Man who Drank the Farm', with thanks to the author. / W.F. Marshall, 'Me an' Me Da' from *Ballads & Verses from Tyrone* (The Talbot Press, Dublin 1929). / Seán Masterson: 'Granum Salis' from *Songs of the Winding Erne*, vol. 2, collected by Seán McElgunn (Lynchprint, Cavan 1994). / Moira O'Neill: 'Never Married' from *Songs of Glens of Antrim* (MacMillan, London 1922). / James Simmons: 'Epigram' from his *Poems 1956–1986* (Gallery Press, Oldcastle 1986). / 'Teddy Bears Picnic', words and music by John W. Bratton and Jimmy Kennedy © 1907, reproduced by permission of B. Feldman & Co. Ltd, London W8 5SW. / Three Anonymous 'Remnants' from *Songs of the Winding Erne*, vol. 2, collected by Seán McElgunn (Lynchprint, Cavan 1994).

Our further thanks to the many kind people who helped bring this collection together, and to Roy Clements in particular. I am especially grateful to Eileen Meharg, Doreen McBride and Sean McElgunn, who have all allowed us to use any material that we found appropriate for this book from their extensive collections of poems, published and unpublished.

Index of Titles and First Lines